The Latino Challenge
to Black America

The Latino Challenge to Black America

by

Earl Ofari Hutchinson

**MID|DLE
PASS|AGE
PRESS**

The Latino Challenge to Black America

Printed in the United States

Publsihed by
Middle Passage Press
5517 Secrest Drive
Los Angeles, California 90043

Designed by Alan Bell

Publisher's Cataloging-in-Publication
(Provided by Quality Books, Inc.)

Hutchinson, Earl Ofari.
    The Latino Challenge to Black America : towards a conversation between African-Americans and Hispanics / by Earl Ofari Hutchinson.
        p. cm.
    Includes bibliographical references and index.
    ISBN-13: 978-1-881032-22-9
    ISBN-10: 1-881032-22-1
    1. African Americans—Relations with Hispanic Americans. 2. Hispanic Americans—Social conditions. 3. African Americans—Social conditions. 4. Social conflict—United States. I. Title.
E185.615.H88 2007   305.868'073
                            QBI07-600132

Table of Contents

The Latino Challenge
to Black America

Introduction

The statement was innocent enough, or so I thought. But the answer I got was unexpected and eye-opening. In 1974 I was part of a small delegation of journalists, artists, and entertainers that toured main land China for three weeks. At lunch the day before the tour ended, I chatted with a delegation member named Miguel. He was a poet from the South Side of Chicago. Since Miguel had a Spanish accent, I assumed that he was Puerto Rican. I was born and raised in Chicago and dimly remembered that there was a Puerto Rican family on my block, and there was one who attended the Catholic school I went to in the early 1960s.

I casually mentioned that to Miguel. He jerked his head and snapped that he wasn't Puerto Rican, he was Mexican. I blurted out, "I didn't know there were Mexicans in Chicago." Miguel frowned and snapped, "You didn't?" What, were you into gangs, or the streets, then?" I was embarrassed and I sheepishly mumbled no, then changed the subject.

Miguel's pithy but agitated response was both a revelation and an education for me. It also revealed much more than just my personal ignorance about Mexicans in Chicago, or equally bad, that, I had insultingly mistook him for a Puerto Rican. Mexicans had been an integral part of Chicago life for decades. On the eve of the 1930s Great Depression there were more than 25,000 Mexicans living on the south side and near the west side of the city. They lived in old, established, and —in keeping with Chicago then—totally segregated neighborhoods, owned businesses, and worked in the stockyards and the steel and auto plants in those years. Chicago had the largest Mexican community in the Midwest. By the 1970s, there were more than 300,000 Mexicans in the city (today there are officially more than a half million).

For all I knew, though, Mexicans might as well have been on the far side of the moon. The Chicago I grew up in was also rigidly segregated, and racial problems were strictly between blacks and whites. The only whites I saw were cops, or a handful of mom and pop grocery store owners. The thought never occurred that there were Mexicans, Puerto Ricans, El Salvadorans, Cubans and Dominicans in Chicago and that they also faced discrimination, and many were poor.

Three decades later, Latinos are no longer a visible blip on the chart in Chicago or in America. In 2002, the Census made it official: Latinos are the top minority in America. That raised the stakes on race relations in America, and it also forced blacks to recognize that racial challenges are now as much a challenge in black and brown as they are black and white. That's a radical departure from the past.

In the year I made that embarrassing statement to Miguel, blacks and Latinos still enjoyed the political honeymoon of the 1960s, a time when there was much talk about and some actual action on black and brown unity, mostly among radical political and activist groups such as the Black Panthers, Young Lords, and the Brown Berets. Neither group wanted to admit that the serious political and cultural differences between blacks and Latinos could crack the facade of unity. The tensions between Latinos and blacks might have continued to smolder under the surface except for several changes.

The assassination of Martin Luther King, Jr. in 1968, the collapse of the civil rights movement, and the self-destruction of the black power movement in the late 1960s brought fragmentation and disillusionment to black organizations. Black leaders, such as King and the black militants, who were willing to extend their vision of change to Latinos, were gone. The leadership vacuum marked the start of the retreat to racial isolation.

During the 1970s, bolstered by affirmative action, greater access to colleges and business support programs, the black middle class grew in size and importance. The number of black elected officials sharply jumped and black political leverage and influence in the Democratic Party increased. Blacks now demanded more affirmative action programs, school integration, business development and corporate advancement. The black middle class did not need or welcome alliances with other ethnic groups.

However, the 1990s presented a new reality. Through massive immigration and higher birth rates, the Latino population soared. But it's not just the numbers. Like blacks, many Latinos have prospered in the professions and business, and have deepened their influence particularly within the Republican Party. Latinos demanded that political and social issues no longer be framed solely in black and white.

The agendas of African-Americans and Latinos have at times drastically diverged and clashed on immigration, political empowerment, bilingual education, and, of course, jobs. The diverging agendas are at times driven by the fear of many blacks that Latinos are getting an unfair boost up at their expense, and by many Latinos that blacks are getting an unfair boost up at their expense.

This has caused much ethnic heartache, especially in Los Angeles, my city. Take just one example: health care. Unlike jail or gang fights, or the battles over immigration and bilingual education (which has been the subject of countless national news articles and TV specials that purport to show an irreparable black and Latino divide), one would think that the last issue which blacks and Latinos would cast a wary eye at each other over would be the struggle for access to affordable health care for the poor.

In December 2006, Susan Kelly, the incoming president of Drew Medical University in South Los Angeles, made the stunning announcement that the school would reach out to Latinos, and that meant recruiting more Latino interns, doctors and, staff, and increasing the number of Latinos on the board of directors. Since its start in the late 1970s, the university has been nationally, even internationally, known as a training and education center for doctors, residents and interns. Its explicit mandate has been to serve the medical needs of poor blacks in Watts. The school was black-run and managed. However, now that Latinos make up the majority of residents in the neighboring area, Latino community leaders demanded a bigger voice in the operation of the university. Kelly (an Australian) flatly said that being white kept her above the fray: "Had the board chosen an African-American, the Latinos would have said, 'You're not listening.' And had they chosen a Latino, the African-Americans would have said, 'You sold us out, our dream is gone.'"

Yet Kelly walked a tightrope, and in the next breath seemed to nod back toward blacks: "I made a promise that I would never advance Latinos at the price of African-Americans." That she felt she had to back-step, at least rhetorically, and smooth any ruffled feathers blacks might have felt at the

school's overt pitch to Latinos, was another sign that black
and Latino relations are touchy and politically sensitive, even
on an issue that ostensibly shouldn't be.

That's even more reason to say at the start: I make no
pretense that this book is an exhaustive or comprehensive
dissection of these complex and engaging issues, the divisions, the conflicts, and the efforts at cooperation between
Latinos and blacks.

I make no claim to delve to the depths of the equally
complex divisions and identity issues between Cubans, Dominicans, El Salvadorans, Mexicans, Guatemalans, Chileans,
and all others who have loosely been lumped into the catchall category of "Latino." There are many other popular and
scholarly works that examine in great detail the emergence
of Latinos as an economic and political force in America, and
more are coming on the market every day.

I certainly do not treat blacks and Latinos as monolithic
in their thinking on race, politics, education, immigration,
and their views on relations between Latinos and blacks.
The opinion on immigration of a conservative black group
such as Project 21 is wildly different than that of the NAACP.
Many Latino community groups have actively worked with
black groups to tackle problems from failing urban schools
to gang violence. There are other Latino groups that prefer
that Latinos go it alone in the fight for immigrant rights and
even civil rights.

I am far more interested in examining the issues and problems that both conflict and unite blacks and Latinos, and in looking at how they see and interpret them through the prism of their experiences. The book is a highly readable, fast paced, cutting edge survey that blends the personal and the analytical, and that ultimately can serve as a guide to navigate race and ethnic relations through 21st Century America. This effort wouldn't have been possible without help. I'd like to thank Barbara Bramwell, Sikivu Hutchinson, Randy Ertll, Ellis Cose, Nicholas Vaca, Alan Bell, and Roberto Novato for their kind and timely support in reading, criticizing, and suggesting vital changes.

I also owe a profound debt of gratitude to Louis Nevaer, President of Hispanic Economics. He suggested that I expand the series of op-ed pieces I did on immigration and other aspects of black and Latino relations over the past five years in my syndicated column into a book exclusively for Spanish language readers and the book market in Mexico and other Latin American countries. That was indeed a challenge, a challenge that ultimately led me to try and understand and make sense out of the Latino challenge to Black America. I owe that to Miguel.

CHAPTER 1

Rising Latino Numbers, Rising Black Fears

I n October 2005, one month after Katrina ripped through New Orleans, a plainly agitated New Orleans Mayor Ray Nagin told a town hall audience, "I can plainly see in your eyes that you want to know, 'How do I take advantage of this incredible opportunity? How do I make sure New Orleans is not overrun with Mexicans?'" He referred to the fear of many blacks that contractors, with the federal government's connivance, would skirt labor laws, snub needy black workers and recruit thousands of unskilled Mexican workers to do the cleanup and reconstruction work in New Orleans and the Gulf Coast.

The remark was insensitive and insulting. And within days an enraged United States Hispanic Chamber of Commerce denounced Nagin: "The Chamber will not allow inappropriate and offensive comments made by Mayor Nagin to deter the hardworking spirit of our community."

The Chamber's denunciation was more than a mere slap at him. It conjured up the positive image of Latinos as productive, taxpaying, law abiding and above all else, hardworking. For years, the Chamber and nearly every major Latino business, political, educational and civil rights group had lobbied hard to sell that image to millions of doubting and skeptical American-born whites and blacks. And now with one mindless crack, Nagin had tarred that image. But observers at the town hall meeting also noted that the mostly black audience applauded his remarks. Their applause, Nagin's quip, and the Chamber's swift outrage told much about the fear, hostility, misconceptions and ambivalence that haunt black and Latino relations in America.

The rising tension that underlay the Chamber's protest of Nagin was probably inevitable after the Census Bureau in 2002 publicly trumpeted that Latinos were now the top minority in the U.S. The news hit black America like a thunderbolt.

Sensing that the Census announcement and the press's seemingly too eager rush to play the news up could ruffle racial feathers, and could be exploited by some to intensify racial friction and ill feelings of blacks toward Latinos, dozens of Latino academics, writers and activists signed an "Open Letter to African-Americans from Latinos." They passionately assured blacks that they would "combat the competitiveness" and "opportunism" of many who would seek to pit Latinos against blacks while minimizing the historic suffering of blacks and displacing them from the front-running spot they still occupied in the struggle for justice and equality. Writer Richard Rodriguez went even further and blasted federal demographers for malice and stupidity for blaring out that Latinos were now the number one minority. He saw this as a virtual conspiracy by the feds to further "trivialize" blacks and equally bad, to marginalize Latinos as a permanent minority.

The criticism from Rodriguez and assurances from the Latino letter signers was a welcomed effort. But it went largely unreported and unnoticed by blacks. Many blacks still complained that they would be shoved even further to the economic and political margin among minorities in the country. The Census report also showed that Latinos were widening their population growth gap on blacks. That gap will grow even wider in the coming years due to the higher birth rate of Latinos and the continued flood of new immigrants, both legal and illegal, from Mexico, El Salvador, Guatemala, Columbia and other Latin American countries.

The reality that blacks will lose even more ground in the numbers comparison to Latinos as fresh waves of immigrants come to America will likely stir more complaints from many blacks. Those complaints rose to a high pitch during the immigration debate in Congress and the mass immigrant rights marches in the streets in March 2006. Though polls showed that blacks were generally more favorable toward illegal immigrants than whites, the polls seemed wildly at odds with the sentiments that many blacks privately expressed on immigration. At the peak of the immigration debate, legions of blacks flooded black talk radio stations and Internet sites with angry comments bashing illegal immigrants. The comments were often little more than thinly disguised attacks on Latinos.

Most civil rights leaders and black Democrats vigorously condemned the ethnic assaults. They publicly backed and embraced the immigrant rights struggle as a crucial and compelling civil rights fight. Yet the dread many blacks have of being bypassed in the eternal battle against poverty and discrimination is not totally groundless. Corporations have leaped over each other to grab a bigger share of Latino consumer dollars and are slowly retreating from affirmative action programs for upwardly-mobile, college-trained black businesspersons and professionals, and are decreasing funding for job and skills training programs for the black poor. The day the Census report was released, the AC Nielson firm, one of the country's top marketing information companies, predicted that retail stores and supermarkets would launch a massive campaign to market their products to Latino buyers.

Since dollars and politics are tightly linked, Republicans and Democrats would radically ramp up their efforts to bag the Latino vote. President Bush understood the crucial importance of the Latino vote better than any other Republican politician. As Texas governor during the 1990s, he adroitly read the political tea leafs. He wined and dined Latino voters, politicians, business leaders and Mexican government officials.

Despite his towering mistakes on many major foreign and domestic policy issues (highest on that list of blunders being the Iraq war), as president he didn't miss a beat in his court of the Latino vote. His tout of Mexico-U.S. relations, championing of relatively liberal immigration reform, and radio broadcasts in broken Spanish washed away some of the bad taste that die-hard Republican opposition to bilingual education and immigrant rights had left in the mouths of Latino voters in California and the Southwest in the mid-1990s. That paid big dividends for him in grabbing the crucial Western and Southwestern states and Florida in both his presidential wins in 2000 and 2004.

Even if Bush hadn't wooed Latino voters, a substantial number of them would still have backed the Republicans.

Polls showed that a sizeable number of Latinos, especially the more than 20 million Latino evangelicals in America, are pro-family values, pro-small business, anti-abortion, and anti-gay rights, and supportive of the military. They are ripe for the GOP line. They also are not tightly bound in the straitjacket of the Democratic Party. In California and Texas there are politically active and influential Latino Republican legislative caucuses. In the 2004 election, Bush nabbed more than one-third of the Latino vote.

· · · · ·

The emergence of Latinos as a force in politics and their rising economic clout forced the Democrats to scramble even harder to match and top the Republicans in the hunt for Latino votes. In the run-up to the 2008 presidential election both parties will spend millions to bump up their share of the Latino vote. Democrats feel no need to make the same effort with blacks, who are already solid Democrats. And in the wake of the Katrina Hurricane debacle that struck New Orleans and the Gulf Cost in 2005, their fury against Bush and the Republicans was even more boundless. But there may be a steep cost to blacks of that one-dimensional support for Democrats.

The Democrats may well spend fewer dollars on black voter registration, and place less emphasis on the vital public policy issues that especially impact poor black communities. That would put blacks in a double bind. If through anger, alienation or distrust of the Democrats, they stay away from the polls in droves in 2008, they doom themselves to be pushed even further to the political edge.

The Democrats are banking that announced their 2008 presidential contenders Barack Obama, Hillary Clinton and John Edwards can energize more black voters, especially the younger voters. They hope that New Mexico governor Bill Richardson, an Hispanic who tossed his hat into the 2008 presidential ring, can do the same with Latino voters. All of the Democratic presidential contenders will sink massive amounts of money as well as expend extensive time and energy trying to sell their campaigns to Latino voters.

Then there's immigration. Whether Congress eventually passes an immigration reform law or not, no matter what kind of bill it is, the issue will still be at or near the top of national debate in 2008. That debate will continue to prick a tender spot with many blacks. They'll continue to blame illegal immigrants for stealing jobs, and for their getting even shorter shrift in the dole-out of shrinking funds for education and heath care. Some blacks, out of fear, anger or desperation, may even flirt with the borderline racially-suspect fringe group, the Minuteman Project.

There is one other concern that engenders more anger and resentment among some blacks and confusion among whites and some Latinos. That is: who should be called and counted in the Census as a Latino? Are Puerto Ricans, Dominicans, Panamanians, Mexicans, Columbians, Venezuelans, Nicaraguans and Brazilians of African ancestry in the United States truly Latinos, and do many of them identify with, and as, Latinos?

Do many of them suffer the same anti-black prejudices and indignities that many native-born blacks suffer in this country? Are they really accepted as equals by white- and lighter-skinned members from their respective countries? "Put bluntly, what does an English-speaking third-generation, upper-class white Cuban American in Florida," ask Latino scholars Marcelo M. Suarez-Orozco and Mariela M. Paez, "have in common with a Maya-speaking recent immigrant from Guatemala?"

They could have easily added that a white, third-generation, upper crust Cuban has virtually nothing in common They could have easily added that a white, third-generation, upper-crust Cuban has virtually nothing in common with the newly arrived Guatemalan. But that same upper-crust Cuban would more likely than not deny the newly-arrived Guatemalan immigrant a business or home loan, and if he or she had the money and skills, employ every scheme imaginable not to rent or sell a home or apartment to him or her in his neighborhood, erect every barrier possible to keep him or her out of a management job in a Cuban-owned business or corporation, solely because of his or her dark skin. Being Latino makes no difference. This is not mere speculation. Countless studies and surveys have documented broad patterns of discrimination by white Cubans against dark-skinned Cubans and blacks in Miami.

Though far too many government officials in Latin American countries still downplay or deny that color discrimination exists in their countries, the harsh fact is that those of African ancestry in Latin American countries wallow at the bottom of the social and economic ladder. This is a strong indictment of the color prejudice against blacks and dark-skinned Indians in Mexico and Latin America.

Yet the Census simply lumps all those from Spanish-speaking countries into the catchall category of "Latino" and made no national or regional distinction between Latinos from various Latin American countries. This generic combining of those who hail from Spanish speaking countries with native-born Latinos insured that "Latinos" would surpass blacks in the American population count.

It also obscures the profound differences in the motive that drives many Spanish-speaking immigrants to this country. It isn't always the eternal search, or maybe even the stereotypical and facile view that says Latino immigrants regard America as their ticket out of poverty and destitution in their own countries. Three million El Salvadorans and 1.5 million Guatemalans had fled from their countries to the

United States during and after the 1980s to escape the civil wars, death squads and harsh military quasi-fascist regimes that claimed thousands of lives in those countries. "Many Salvadoran immigrants were already political activists and refugees," notes Randy Ertll, a second generation El Salvadoran in Los Angeles and director of *El Centro de Accion*, a social service agency in Pasadena, California. "They knew how to mobilize people and many established their own community organizations." The organizations he mentioned are *El Rescate*, Central American Resource Center, and *Clinica Romero*. These organizations have provided services to blacks as well as El Salvadoran and other Central American immigrants.

This made a difference in the manner in which blacks have related to El Salvadorans and Guatemalans in Los Angeles. When Los Angeles Police SWAT officers stormed a business during a hostage standoff in South L.A. in July 2005, and killed three-year-old Suzie Pena, the daughter of El Salvadoran immigrants, blacks held candlelight vigils and demonstrations against the police killing.

The interaction between blacks and El Salvadorans in the schools, on the streets, and in the case of the Pena killing, in protests over alleged police abuse, has fostered a relationship that can be characterized by a mix of passivity, indifference, and in some cases cooperation rather than friction. In Los Angeles, the tens of thousands of Guatemalan and El

Salvadoran refugees and immigrants have not as yet been particularly vocal or visible in pushing demands for greater political power, more El Salvadoran teachers and administrators in the schools, or more public sector jobs. These have been flash-point areas of friction between some blacks and Mexican-Americans.

There is also little evidence that El Salvadoran gangs (and there are reportedly hundreds of El Salvadoran gang members in the city), have fought battles with black gangs over the drug trade or turf control. Nor has there been any evidence that El Salvadoran prison gangs have precipitated the violence against blacks in the prison brawls that have wracked L.A. County jails and California prisons since the mid-1990s. This is another reason to be cautious of the generic lumping of all Latinos in the category of protagonist to blacks.

• • • • •

In the 1980s, Puerto Rican author Felix M. Padilla was one of the first to protest the labeling of Mexicans, Puerto Ricans, Cubans, Dominicans, and others from Spanish speaking countries under the generic term "Latinos." Padilla noted that a homogeneous Latino culture has never existed in Latin America, and it certainly doesn't exist in the Untied States. The cultural differences and historical development are so radically different between Puerto Ricans and

Mexicans in this country that it renders absurd the stuffing of both groups under the term "Latino."

There are also major differences in relations between blacks and "Latinos" in different parts of the country. Blacks and Puerto Ricans in Chicago and New York City have had a long, close and personal history of working and living together in neighborhoods and barrios. Puerto Rican and black elected officials, educators and community activists in both cities have cooperated to get more blacks and Puerto Ricans elected in city elections, in the battles for school improvement, and increased neighborhood services. In November 1983, Harold Washington effusively thanked Hispanic leaders for putting him over the top in the Chicago mayor's race.

The Young Lords, a radical Puerto Rican activist group, and the Black Panther Party conducted joint marches and protests against police and landlord abuses during the late 1960s. A major reason for the closer affinity between blacks and Puerto Ricans between than blacks and Mexicans (and then between blacks and first-generation white Cubans) is part racial and part economic. A significant number of Puerto Ricans are black, or mixed race (black and white), and are more likely to suffer the same intense anti-black racial abuses as black Americans, and they have the highest poverty rate among Latino groups.

Even Linda Chavez, a conservative Republican writer and ideologue who attacks any hint of racial one-upmanship by minorities, points squarely to race as a big reason for the huge lag of Puerto Ricans behind Mexican-Americans and Cuban-Americans in income and education. She brands it the "Puerto Rican exception."

That doesn't mean that there aren't tensions and even conflicts between blacks and Puerto Ricans. "For Hispanics in New York, relations with native blacks are deeply ambivalent, " says sociologist Phillip Kasinitz, "and matters aren't helped when scholars use the relative gains of dark-skinned immigrants to point up the alleged failure of native blacks." In *Growing Up Puerto Rican,* a collection of street people, laborers, domestics, gang members, students and activists tell of their experiences in New York's barrios. They also talk about their relations with blacks: the friendships, conflicts, problems and emotional feelings they have with and toward them. The ambivalence and at times hostility is there, but so is the willingness to cooperate on some political and educational issues.

• • • • •

That same ambivalence has been present in relations between blacks and Mexicans or Mexican-Americans in Texas. But their relations have not been marred by the kinds of tensions and at times violent strife that have occurred between blacks and Cubans in Miami and blacks and Mexicans in Los Angeles. That was apparent during the hotly contested mayoral race in Houston in 2001. The city's black mayor, Lee Brown, held off a strong challenge from Houston city councilman Orlando Sanchez, who would have been Houston's first Latino mayo, had he been elected. The likelihood was great that that would have happened had Sanchez gotten total support from Latino voters.

But, he didn't get that. Brown was endorsed by nearly one hundred Latino business and political leaders, and thirty percent of Latinos backed him. It was no mystery why. Brown actively courted Latino voters, and pledged that he'd make City Hall and his administration inclusive. Enough Latino voters, and business and political leaders believed him, and they helped put him over the top. That wouldn't have happened if there had been a history of rancor and distrust between blacks and Latinos in Houston and the state.

However, the Census declaration that Latinos had edged blacks out of the top spot among minorities in America was more than a numbers game. The greater the Latino population, the greater was the incentive for advertisers to spend millions of dollars courting Latino consumers, via ads in Latino publications and on radio and TV stations. The numbers further guaranteed that Republicans and Democrats would drastically hike the dollars they'd spend in 2008 to nab more of the Latino vote. That potentially could mean even fewer dollars they'd spend on ads in the black media on voter education and registration drives to ramp up the black vote.

There's also the ever-present and seeming intractable problem of the stereotyped image that many Latinos, especially those newly arrived in America, have of blacks. Duke University researchers found that recent Latino immigrants in Durham, North Carolina spouted the same age-old stereotyped views about blacks that whites did. A majority said they were lazy and untrustworthy. The irony is that whites by a far smaller margin than Latinos said negative things about blacks. It appeared from that finding that whites weren't the culprits in feeding negative attitudes about blacks to Latinos. The obvious conclusion was that the Latinos that expressed racist attitudes brought them from their countries. "Will blacks find that they must not only make demands on whites for continued progress," Paula D. McClain (who led the research study) worriedly asked, "but also mount a fight on another front against Latinos?" Many Latinos wonder out loud the same thing, and some Latino writers and political leaders have feverishly sought an answer to that question from their perspective.

That is the dismaying and still unanswered question that hovers like a dark cloud over black and Latino relations in America. It's clear that the anxiety and resentment of some blacks toward Latinos for being edged out of the top ethnic spot in America won't go away. But the reality is that Latinos are drastically changing America's ethnic face. This change presents a new, at times unnerving and conflicting, but potentially dynamic and energizing challenge to black America.

CHAPTER 2

Stereotypes Drive Black and Latino Conflicts

Achagrined Patricia Olamendi had to swallow her words after she "offered apologies on behalf of my government." The apology was for— and, she thought, on behalf of—then Mexican President Vicente Fox. The President had just created a bit of an international incident and ignited a storm of protest from many American blacks with his quip on May 15, 2005 in a speech in the Mexican seacoast town of Puerto Vallarta praising Mexicans for their dignity and hard work ethic. But then he added that these are the jobs that blacks won't work.

A day later Fox's spokesperson Ruben Aguilar quickly rebuked the Assistant Foreign Secretary. He emphatically said that Olamendi was speaking for herself and not for Fox. The rebuke and the non-apology angered Reverend Jesse Jackson. He jumped on a plane to Mexico City to demand that Fox apologize to blacks.

Following a well-publicized talk and photo-op session with Jackson a few days later, Fox apologized. That was enough for Jackson. He absolved the President of any racial animus and said that he was trying to correct his mistake. That wasn't quite enough for the Reverend Al Sharpton. He wanted Fox to conduct a full-blown dialogue presumably with himself and other blacks on race. Soon after Jackson's visit to Fox, Sharpton got on another plane to the Mexican capital to try to prod Fox into conducting that dialogue. Fox politely met with Sharpton and the two men held yet another smiling photo-op session. And that's where it ended. There would be no dialogue, at least one that was led by Fox.

However, the issue and the flap didn't quite blow over. The Congressional Hispanic Caucus, the top Mexican-American legal and civil rights groups, Mexican American Legal Defense and Education Fund (MALDEF), the National Council of La Raza, and the League of United Latin American Citizens (LULAC) also scurried to denounce Fox's remarks. They instantly understood the severe harm that the remark could do to the fragile relations between blacks and

Latinos. "Your words have the potential to alienate not just African-Americans but also Mexican-Americans," the CHC somberly warned. The hint that Fox's words could have a detrimental affect on Mexican-Americans was the CHC's way of saying that many Latinos were just as concerned about building positive relations with blacks.

Many are concerned about that, but many Mexicans openly and some Mexican-Americans privately agreed with Fox. They insisted that Mexican immigrants would work the hardest, dirtiest, lowest paying jobs that blacks won't work. And some even less charitably claimed that blacks wouldn't work these jobs because they are lazy and slothful.

That belief is crude, false, and racist. But it also reflects a much bigger problem. Relations between blacks and Latinos are rife with myths and misconceptions. It's partly cultural and partly economic. Mexican TV viewers are fed a daily diet of American sitcoms and gangster shoot-em-ups in which blacks are portrayed as clowns, buffoons and crooks. The programs are beamed to Mexico and other countries on cable and satellite networks.

An entire generation of Mexican school children (and many adults) grew up reading the popular comic strip series that mimicked the exploits of Memin Pinguin. Memin had grossly distorted monkey-like features, a bald head and big ears. His mother was fat, bandanna wearing mammy. It was the classic racist mammy image of black female domestics.

The difference was that she wasn't a domestic. She wore her bandanna around their house.

Pinguin and his mother lived in a ramshackle house in one of the poorest barrios in Mexico City. Writer Yolanda Vargas created the series, which ran from 1963 until 1977. The Memin Pinguin series was so popular that decades after the series was discontinued fan clubs continued to sprout up on both sides of the border. The comic books are still wildly popular collectors' items and continue to be much discussed and much read. Emoe de la Parra, Vargas' daughter, was unfazed by the controversy. In a radio interview with Mexico's City's W Radio, she was defiantly unapologetic about the racist implications of the series: "I'm very surprised that it has raised concerns, that it has bothered people and that it even has political relevance in negative terms."

Many Mexicans refer to dark-skinned persons, both Mexican and non-Mexican, as *negritos* or little black people. This is not seen as racist or offensive. It is regarded as a term of affection, even endearment. A popular afternoon *telenovela* on Mexican TV in 2005 had a comedian in blackface chasing after light-complexioned actresses in skimpy outfits. Ads have featured Mexicans in Afros, black face, and distorted features. The most popular screen stars in film and on TV, and the models featured on magazines and billboards, are white or fair skinned with sandy or blond hair. "Racism is very deeply ingrained here, but no one accepts that fact," said

Sergio Aguayo, a Mexican human rights activist. "The paradigm of beauty is white skin and blue eyes."

During an extended stay in Mexico, a few years ago, I lived with a well-to-do Mexican family. Family members routinely asked if my son was into gangs and drugs (he was a college student at the time). I did not regard this as insensitive or even racist. I chalked it up in part to the one-dimensional depiction of blacks on many TV shows, in movies, and in newscasts out of America that are beamed worldwide.

· · · · ·

The other part I chalked up to the treatment of blacks in Mexico. They make up about two percent of the population. But that's only a rough estimate. The Mexican government has propagated the myth of a color-blind society and has never designated any particular racial categories. But Mexico is one of the most rabidly color-conscious of societies. Even while Mexican writers and politician's protest in articles against American racism, many Mexicans are quick to boast of differences in skin color among their own family members.

It's no accident that current Mexican President Felipe Calderon, Fox, and most of Mexico's past presidents, top officials, business leaders, educators and government leaders are Castellan Spanish; that is, of European ancestry or extremely fair skinned. They routinely tout their bloodlines from Spain (Fox's mother is from Spain). A Mexican-American friend made me acutely aware of the rigid caste and class differences in the country and how both are firmly tied to skin color. He urged me to note who is doing the hardest and dirtiest work in restaurants and hotels, and who the beggars and peddlers on the streets are. They are overwhelmingly dark, and in most cases have pronounced Indian features.

The blond and blue-eyed Western standard of beauty, culture, and sophistication has been held up as the supreme global standard of beauty to emulate in other places as well as Mexico and throughout Latin America. The models, actors and actresses on American and European TV shows, in films, filling magazine, and media fill the screens and ads are lithe, blond or brunette. The light-skinned, straight-haired, keen-featured beauty standard is commercialized and peddled as a prime commodity in the U.S., too.

The overwhelming majority of Latino talk show hosts, ad models, and the stars on the *telenovelas* on American Spanish language TV stations are white or fair-skinned. In 2000, several thousand Latino members of the Screen Actors Guild told survey takers that dark skin was a liability for a Latino actor or actress trying to get a part or a spot in a Spanish language TV production. That's not likely to change any time soon if economics and stereotypes drive viewer tastes and the station's corporate owner's preferences.

Former CEO and president of *Univision* Henry Cisneros inadvertently confirmed that fact when an inquiring writer challenged him on his station's and the industries' color-coded racially skewed hiring practices by. He didn't blanche: "Without them (the *telenovelas),* we'd be out of business." Cisneros admitted that diversity was a concern of the station owners and promised that they'd take a close look at their practices. If bottom line profits are the main thing that they look at, and they are, in making decisions on the skin color of who Spanish language TV viewers see on the little screen, that promise will remain just that, an unkept promise.

Writer and social critic Marita Golden in her book *Don't Play in the Sun* branded this slavish emulation of European standards as the global color complex: "Africans, Asians, Indians use skin lighteners and believe that that their lives will be improved if their skin is lighter. Light skin equals privilege, power, and influence." This is a brutal, sweeping, and perhaps over-the-top criticism since many dark skinned peoples in Latin America and Africa rejects the notion that light skin or white skin automatically means beauty and power, and take pride in their color and ancestry. The indisputable truth, though, is that the majority of those in power tend to be white or lighter-skinned in Latin America.

• • • • •

F ox's remark that blacks won't work the jobs that Mexicans will work created a flap among few Mexicans. In truth his gibe was more than a deliberate mean-spirited racial slur of blacks. It simply reflected longstanding language use and assumptions many Mexicans have about American blacks, and their view of the racial and economic conditions in the United States. Gilberto Rincon, President of the National Council to Prevent Discrimination, noted that a report on racism in Mexico was released prior to Fox's statement. That was seen as a sign that the government was grudgingly beginning to acknowledge that race did matter in Mexican affairs. Yet race stratification in Mexico is no different than in other Latin American countries. That stratification has spelled social and economic misery for many blacks in those countries. According to government reports issued by the governments of Columbia, Guatemala, Uruguay and Brazil in the late 1990s, blacks in these countries are the poorest and suffer the greatest health and education disparities. In Nicaragua, the greatest concentration of blacks is in the impoverished Caribbean coastal region of the country. The blacks there have the least access to potable water of other groups.

The racial and class hierarchy and privilege in these countries has had direct and severe implications for race and ethnic relations in America. If many Hispanic immigrants who are freshly arrived in the U.S. thought of themselves as white in their countries of origin, they think of themselves as white in the U.S. That includes identification with the values and standards they perceive are held by white Americans.

Their identification with whites intensifies when they swap the citizenship in their countries for American citizenship. In 2000, foreign-born Latino immigrants who became citizens were more likely to check the "white" box on the Census form than non-citizens. The non-citizens were more likely to check the "some other race" box. That was a vague but probably polite euphemism for black. The non-citizens were also much more likely to be less educated and poorer than their "white" immigrant counterparts. In other words, the class and race privilege and attitudes that reign south of the border are easily transferable to the north. Sonya Tafoya, a Pew Hispanic Center researcher, analyzed the racial schisms in the white versus non-white designations of immigrants and noted that, "Race goes beyond physical characteristics and skin color." If the willingness of so many foreign-born Latinos to claim whiteness for themselves is any sign, it doesn't go too much beyond color. Even worse, it may not go beyond discrimination.

In Mexico and the other Latin American countries there is no official ban on employment discrimination. Classified ads in magazine and newspapers are filled with requests for job applicants who are young and beautiful, and though it's unstated, the lighter and more fair-skinned, the better. In the

1990s the guerrilla war in Chiapas, and land battles between Indian groups and government officials in other parts of the country, have drawn national and international attention. This forced the government to make minimal reforms to deal with the economic and racial ill-treatment of the Indians. The government has not shown the same level of sensitivity and enlightenment toward its black population. They remain just as invisible and just as low on the country's social and economic totem pole.

Bobby Vaughn, a cultural anthropologist and leading expert of Afro-Mexican life and culture, observed, "There is a general recognition that blacks (in Mexico) are at the bottom of the social scale in many ways." The ways include poor underserved schools, and lack of decent roads and public services in their enclaves in the states of Guerrero, Oaxaca and Vera Cruz, harassment by police, the lack of business and professional opportunities, and the refusal of officials to recognize the cultural contributions in music, art and dance of Afro-Mexicans. And since most Mexicans have little opportunity to interact with prominent blacks in business, the professions and politics, that cultural isolation helps reinforce the negative stereotypes of Mexicans of African ancestry.

Fox, Mexican officials and most Mexicans have never deliberately targeted African-Americans for denigration because of bigotry, maliciousness, or out of plain insensitivity. They are not enough of a factor in the country's politics or

the daily lives of Mexicans for that. A racial and class hierarchy based on skin color and economic standing remains a
long-standing and disturbing social and economic fact of life
in Mexico, and in nearly all other Latin American countries.
The attitudes and stereotypes about dark skin, and more particularly black Americans, are routinely and even daily reinforced by negative media depictions of blacks. Sadly, many
immigrants transport those negative racial attitudes with
them to America. This adds yet another complex and troubling element to black and Latino relations. It also insures
that many blacks and Latinos will continue to see each other
through the prism of skewed and warped stereotypes.

CHAPTER 3

Warped Perceptions in Black and Brown

N icolas Vaca in his compelling book on the twists and turns of black and Latino relations in America, *Presumed Alliance,* lists seven axioms that will profoundly change how Latinos and blacks see and deal with each other now and in the future. Axiom Number two states that Latinos have a history of oppression. He's right. There is a long history of oppression. Vaca and other writers have largely avoided engaging in the my-suffering-is-greater-than-yours. It's a no-win tit-for-tat with blacks. Mexicans and other Latino immigrants feel that they've faced discrimination in the U.S. that has been every bit as harsh as that of blacks. This discrimination has been pitiless. In decades past, Mexican immigrants were harshly exploited as cheap labor in mines, factories, and the fields of the Southwest.

When the U.S. government terminated the two-decade-long Bracero program in 1960 in which Mexico supplied contract labor to mostly American agribusiness growers, Mexicans instantly became labor expendables. The INS launched "Operation Wetback" sweeps and deportations. Thousands were summarily kicked out of the country. The ugly remnant of that neglect and violence today is the reported rise in incidents of taunts, harassment, and physical attacks against some Latino immigrants throughout the country, not to mention the hundreds of illegal immigrants who have been maimed, abused, and have even perished in crossings at the U.S.-Mexican border. The upswing in violence is almost certainly attributable to the mania over the immigration reform battle.

Yet many Mexicans and other Latin American immigrants overcame the vicious racial exclusion and economic exploitation, and managed to build thriving businesses and climb up the professional ladder in America.

On the other hand, despite being in America for centuries, many blacks still remain trapped in a hopeless morass of poverty, crime, violence, drugs and family deterioration. The newer immigrants accuse blacks of demanding expensive and wasteful government programs, rather than emphasizing self-help and personal initiative to draw themselves out of their economic misery.

Few immigrants say it publicly, but privately some believe that blacks have stagnated because of apathy, laziness, low self-esteem and poor discipline. Even Nation of Islam leader Louis Farrakhan, in his seminal address at the Million Man March in October 1995, after chastising blacks to uplift themselves and their communities pointed a glowing finger at Mexicans as an example of immigrants who are moving forward in America, even if many of them came here illegally.

Farrakhan likes to occasionally sprinkle his talks with references to the spectacular business and professional success of many Asian, Latino and West Indian immigrants. He simply echoed the view of many immigrants who demand to know why blacks haven't done the same.

Measuring black gains against recent non-white immigrants presents a false and skewed picture. The Cubans, Vietnamese, Koreans, West Indians, and many immigrants who came from Mexico and other Latin American countries come from nearly homogeneous countries with the same language, culture, traditions and family continuity. In spite of the racist violence and exclusion against earlier generations of Mexican and other Latino immigrants, they were still immigrants. Blacks were chattel slaves in the United States, and were imported into Mexico, Cuba, and the Dominican Republic (Santo Domingo) as slaves as well. The difference is crucial. The slave planters maintained iron control through military force, economic domination and the ruthless obliteration of African culture and language. They shattered family ties and fostered rivalries and divisions. They twisted science and religion to construct the powerful mythology of black inferiority.

Emancipation did not heal the traumatic psychic scars of slavery. The massive campaign of terror and violence by the former planters and unyielding segregation laws stripped blacks of political rights and reduced them to economic outcasts for a century after the formal end of slavery in 1865, or well into the mid 20th century. When the civil rights movement demolished the walls of legal segregation, blacks were still handicapped. They lacked capital, credit, trade and professional associations and business networks to take full advantage of the expanding opportunities in business and the professions.

• • • • •

This was not true for many non-white immigrants, and that includes West Indians. They possessed job skills, education, business and professional training, and in many cases were able to secure capital and credit from banks. Many of those who didn't have access to bank financing had alternative funding sources.

The Koreans used a rotating credit system called *Kye*. The West Indians used the *isusu* system to pool their savings for investment. The Cubans and Vietnamese relied on ethnic loyalty to carve out "protected markets" to sell and supply their ethnic products, foods and services that white businesses ignored. Each group avoided high labor costs by employing labor from their own ethnic group. They accumulated capital and credit. They expanded and diversified their markets. They provided jobs, training and improved services in their communities.

Meanwhile, African-Americans had no protected markets. White businesses offered the same goods and services at lower costs than black merchants. With the exception of insurance and banking, black businesses were relegated to the economic fringe. They were generally poorly capitalized mom and pop stores, catering, beauty and barbershops that provided no employment, little training and economic return to black neighborhoods.

This sharply contrasts with the way the banks, mortgage lenders and even the federal government has dealt with the wave of immigrants from Mexico since the 1990s. They have sniffed dollars in their numbers and have sought to cash in on them. Bank of America and Wells Fargo Bank provide home and business loans, credit cards, and make it easier to send money directly back to Mexico without producing a social security card. Anti-immigration groups have called this an outrageous example of the government turning a blind eye toward lawbreaking, in this case ignoring the fact that many of those who in the banks, saving and loans institutions, and the government are helping are illegal immigrants. Nonetheless, the government and the banks merely regard this as both good business and smart politics. They recognize that illegal immigrants in most cases are here to stay and that they're dollars are as good as those of any legal citizen.

That points to the crucial role federal and local governments played in making possible the much-vaunted economic miracle of some Latino immigrants. The Kennedy administration officially welcomed with open arms the first wave of Cuban refugees in the early 1960s. Congress eagerly appropriated ten million dollars for their transportation and resettlement. During the next decade, the government-subsidized Cuban Refugee Program shelled out millions more for welfare and family income subsidies, business loans and grants, health care services, jobs, and transportation expenses. The final tab for the program came to nearly a billion dollars from 1961 to 1973. The money exclusively subsidized Cuban immigrant resettlement and adjustment support.

The Cubans were hardly dirt-poor *campesinos* in the first place. Many were former wealthy landowners. Seventy percent had worked in the professions, trades or operated businesses. Forty percent were college educated. In Cuba, eighty percent had earned more than the average income. And Florida passed laws that allowed them to be re-certified and practice their professions and trades in the U.S. Miami-Dade County parceled out government contracts to Cuban owned firms, while Dade County labeled the county officially bilingual.

Despite media attention and public panic over the criminals and "misfits" who arrived during the Mariel boatlift in 1980, the federal government continued to provide most with housing and relocation subsidies. More than thirty percent of the refugees were employed by Cuban businesses. Propelled by American tax dollars, the Cuban economic miracle has certainly been impressive. The billions in total assets of Cuban-owned banks in Miami exceed the combined assets of all the black-owned banks in America.

There was one other big reason for that miracle. The Cubans and the post-1960s wave of immigrants came after the major civil rights battles broke down the barriers of legal segregation. The rash of anti-discrimination laws and affirmative action programs made discrimination and public displays of overt racism legally and politically unacceptable in America.

"Most Asian-Americans would not be here in America today, but for the civil rights movement led by African-Americans that resulted in the change to racist immigration quotas." Though Stewart Kwoh, Executive Director of the

Asian Pacific American Legal Center of Southern California, referred specifically to Asian immigrants, the Cubans and the other post-civil-rights-era immigrants from Latin American countries owe the same outsized debt to the civil rights movement. Not only did it help ease their entrance and increase the degree of acceptance they found in America, it also helped ease their march up the social and economic steps in America.

· · · · ·

This fact has not done much to smooth relations between many blacks and Cubans in Miami. Miami is and has been, since the late 1980s, a city run by Cubans, that is, white Cubans. Black Cubans make up less than ten percent of the city's Cuban population. The majority of the city commissioners are Cuban. The mayors of Miami have been Cuban. Spanish is more likely to be heard on the city's streets than English. And Miami is still a segregated city, though not by law, but by custom, class and ethnicity. There is very little mixture of any kind between blacks—and that includes black Cubans, —and white Cubans.

The myths and misconceptions that each group has had about the other have been a major cause of the violence that tore Miami in the 1980s when mostly white Cuban cops were accused of (and in some cases tried for) killing and beating blacks, and the continued charge by blacks of job and housing discrimination against them by Cuban landlords and business owners. That fueled even greater black frustration over their diminishing political and economic force and their decreasing population numbers in the city.

The negative experiences that have colored relations between many white Cubans and many blacks can be viewed though the window of the experiences of Joel Ruiz and Achmed Valdes. The two young men fled Cuba in 1994. Ruiz is black. Valdes is white. The two grew up in the same neighborhood in Havana, went to the same schools, played together and hung out together.

While color is still a subtle and underlying problem that many blacks face in Cuba, with many top jobs and positions in government and major industries held by white Cubans, Ruiz did not encounter the kind of racial hostility in Cuba that he has in Miami, not only from whites, but from white Cubans. That's not because he's black and Cuban but because he's black. Valdes did express the same negative views toward blacks in Cuba that he has in Miami. But after a few years here, he openly told an interviewer in 2000 that he thought blacks were delinquent and dangerous and that they hate whites. That sentiment is no different than what some other white Cubans have said and believe about blacks.

It's also no different than what many non-Latino whites have said and believed for decades about blacks. Even worse, the casual acceptance by many white Cubans of those racial attitudes came at a time in the early 1960s when white Cuban' skin color gave them an advantage and even privilege. Then Miami National Urban League director James Whitehead noted that when blacks were still legally segregated in Miami, white Cubans were not.

At the time of the interview, Valdes lived in a white neighborhood. He socialized and played soccer exclusively with white Cubans. Ruiz in turn lived in a black neighborhood, and his friends were either black Cubans or African-Americans. The one and only time Valdes visited Ruiz at his home, he and his wife said they were repelled by the houses and the neighborhood. "Maybe it's just because for us, that world is unknown, but we felt uncomfortable."

He hastened to add that he did not consider himself a racist, or that his wariness toward blacks had a racial tinge. His caution and even ill-will toward blacks was merely the normal way that blacks and Cubans related to each other in Miami. He even had some advice for Ruiz and his choice to live in a black neighborhood, and adopt the black American lifestyle: "If I were him, I would get out of there and forget about everybody else's problems and begin my own life. If he stays, it's because he wants to." Valdes didn't acknowledge or maybe even realize that Ruiz preferred to live in an all-black neighborhood because the hostility and sense of rejection coming from both whites and white Cubans was so great that

that neighborhood was the only place he felt comfortable and accepted.

Ruiz did not criticize Valdes when told of his negative views of blacks. He inadvertently confirmed the deep-seated prejudices that some white Cubans cling too: "I am sure he is talking about American blacks." He probably was right about Valdes, though given the social distance that white Cubans have kept from blacks, as well as from black Cubans such as Ruiz, it was a fine distinction to say the least.

In fact, a few hundred miles to the north in Tampa, white and black Cubans still carefully preserved that distance even as Ruiz mused over his friend's words. On the one hundredth anniversary in 2000 of the founding of Circulo Cubano, the mutual aid society that served white Cubans, and Union Marti-Maceo, the mutual aid society that served black Cubans, the two groups celebrated the occasion with separate celebrations. Their memberships were still separate.

Miami has been an urban microcosm of the competing and at times antagonistic, or simply indifferent, relations between blacks and Cubans, with much of the blame for the bad blood between the two attributed to the bigotry of white Cubans in Miami. The bigotry of other Latinos against blacks in other places also contributed.

• • • • •

Ethnic insensitivity, however, is not a one-way street. Blacks have little understanding of the political repression and economic destitution that drove many Mexican, Cuban, El Salvadoran, Dominican and other Latin-American immigrants to seek refuge in the United States. Many have fled from civil strife, massive land dislocations, the chronic lack of industry, and in Mexico, an exploding population crisis. The Mexican economic and population crisis has been the single greatest cause of the post-2000 influx of Latino immigrants to the U.S. The number of Mexicans in the U.S. far exceeds the number of Puerto Ricans, Cubans, and El Salvadorans in the country. Mexicans make up close to sixty percent of Latinos in America. The Mexican population's upward leap, and the failure of the government and private industry to provide jobs to keep pace with the increase has propelled the rush of thousands more Mexicans to the U.S. That won't ease anytime soon. The estimate is that Mexico's population will grow by one million per year for the next three decades.

There is no government safety net in the country for Mexico's unemployed and landless. Mexican immigrants to the U.S. face the daunting problem of readjusting to a strange culture, customs and language. They also live in constant fear of being discovered by the INS, police and other government authorities and sent home. Fox made his intemperate remark in May 2005 about Mexicans willing to work hard not to demean blacks but to slam Bush and Congress for their "get tough" crack-down on illegal immigration. Bush had just signed a law to make it harder for illegal immigrants to get drivers' licenses and to build a wall along the Mexican–U.S. border.

Many blacks minimize the suffering and plight of poor Mexican immigrants. They note that Latinos (and other non-whites) did not experience chattel slavery and its legacy. Their family and ethnic cohesion was not ruptured. They were not color-stamped with the badge of inferiority. To them, this is tantamount to a racial pass that makes it much easier for Latino immigrants to secure business loans, credit, access to education and the professions than blacks.

Many blacks take sole credit for the civil rights victories of the 1960s that broke the back of legal segregation, and shattered the barriers in corporations and professions to minority advancement. This made it much easier for many Latino immigrants to gain a higher degree of acceptance than might have been the case if legal segregation was still the law of the land rather than simply a terrible fact of life for many non-whites.

Yet, that doesn't mean that the success that many Latino immigrants have had has come at the expense of the black struggle and sacrifice, or that they occupy a far higher place in American society, or even that they are arrogant and opportunistic hypocrites who refuse to give credit to blacks for their struggle. Many Latinos, though, are unaware of the history of that struggle and the depth of black suffering in that history.

The view that only blacks struggled for civil rights is a terribly faulty reading of history. Mexicans filed lawsuits against school and housing segregation, staged strikes at plants and factories for better job conditions and for union and civil rights for decades before the 1960s. The ferocious battle that mostly Mexican farmworkers waged in the 1950s and 1960s against the growers for wages, union and civil rights was every bit as vital to the success of labor organizing as union struggles in Northern industries.

The significance of that wasn't lost on Dr. Martin Luther King, Jr. In 1967, he sent a moving and impassioned letter to farmworker union president Cesar Chavez when he was jailed following a protest action in California's central valley. King's top aide, Ralph Abernathy, went further and walked side-by-side with Chavez in a farmworker protest march. In 1970, Coretta Scott King visited Chavez in jail after another protest march. Chavez was profoundly grateful for the support he got from King. Every chance he got, he praised King as his mentor, as the man who was his greatest inspiration. Chavez picked a King day celebration in 1970 to shower even more praise on King: "The United Farmworkers are dedicated to carrying on the dream of Martin Luther King Jr. for building the union. "

• • • • •

The mutual admiration that Chavez and King held for each other provided the often missing link between the civil rights movement and the movement of Latino immigrants for economic and social justice. But it did not make blacks totally immune from the vicious stereotypes and negative typecasting of Mexicans that are still entombed in the belief systems of many Americans.

That was glaringly and troublingly apparent in the firestorm that the late pro football legend and many time pro bowl tackle Reggie White ignited in March 25, 1998 when he addressed the Wisconsin State Assembly. White was not just another superstar pro jock, he was also an ordained minister, and widely respected for his ministry and work with young people. White was also a man of very pronounced views, and he was not shy about making those views publicly known. Even the legislators who were used to the rough-and-tumble give-and-take of legislative debate were not prepared for what White had to say.

In a rambling hour-long talk, he touched on nearly every imaginable hot-button racial and social theme that included racial family breakup, gang violence, and of course, race relations. The shocker, though, was White's lambasting of gays. That drew gasps and touched off protest from gay rights groups. It also cost him a potential lucrative spot on TV. CBS Sports officials quickly announced that they dropped White from consideration as a network commentator.

However, lost in the furor over White's gay bashing remarks was White's crack about Hispanics: "Hispanics are gifted in family structure. You can see a Hispanic person and they can put 20 or 30 people in one home." If White had simply stopped at praising Hispanics for emphasizing strong family ties and values, the remark would have been valid, even praiseworthy, and would have passed under the public radarscope. But in falsely quantifying family strengths and slapping a number on it—ridiculously large number at that—White bought into a popular stereotype. It conjured images of dirt-poor Latinos stuffed into ramshackle homes with dozens of children crammed into a few rooms. It was a short leap from that to the stereotype of Mexicans as sexually loose, having unlimited numbers of babies, flooding the schools, packing workplaces, and bankrupting public services.

In his blast at Fox for his remark on immigration and jobs, Sharpton also reflected the common view held by many blacks that Latinos are an economic threat: "We need to deal with the fact that there has been an inordinate amount of tension where people have come across the border for almost slave wages, competing with Latinos and blacks." Sharpton rammed the point home by describing illegal immigration as a 21st century slave trade. That dredged up the negative images of flocks of uneducated, poor Mexicans invading the U.S.

Latino activists have waged a furious battle for decades

against that image as well as against the depiction of Latinos as lazy, immoral, crime-prone, drug dealers, illegal aliens, service workers, and mothers with packs of ragged children. Those images constitute stereotypes that TV and Hollywood have done much to propagate.

Two studies by the National Association of Hispanic Journalists and University of Michigan researchers in 2003 found that Latinos were even more grossly underrepresented on network TV shows than blacks. But it was still the stereotypes that rankled most. The standard checklist of negative typecasting of Latinos remained unchanged. The men were "greasers" and "banditos." Latinas were "frilly senoritas" and "volcanic temptresses." Latino families were "unintelligent," "passive," "deviant" and "dependent."

• • • • •

Hector Flores, President of the League of United Latin American Citizens, pointed to the public damage that stereotypes have wreaked in poisoning ethnic relations, stoking the racial fires and reinforcing the destructive images of Latinos among many Americans, including many blacks. He quickly made the connection between such portrayals and images and the damage to the Latino image that drives the fears, misperceptions and even hatreds of many Americans toward Latinos, especially recent immigrants. "Now more than ever, immigrants are placed under intense scrutiny by others in America."

Many blacks have been forced by the competition with them over jobs, in the schools and for neighborhood services to scrutinize more closely illegal immigrant and have connected illegal immigration with poverty, violence and unwashed multitudes who have elbowed them out of jobs and even their neighborhoods. Popular black TV host and author Tony Brown was adamant that blacks were paying higher taxes to subsidize not only welfare benefits for illegal immigrants, but also for the businesses that hire them.

Brown was on shaky ground on both counts. Studies have shown that illegal immigrants actually pay more in taxes and get less in benefits than native-born Americans and even legal immigrants. This, however, doesn't change the perception and even encoded stereotypes that Latinos are harming black communities. In a press statement in 2004, Project 21, a Washington, D.C. black Republican group, went even further and flatly charged that illegal immigrants were "bursting" the public schools, "overflowing" the state prisons and dragging down wages for blacks.

The group managed to tick off the common litany of stereotypes, myths and misconceptions that many blacks routinely toss out about Latino immigrants. When those beliefs and sentiments rudely force their way and badly taint the way blacks and Latinos see each other, it guarantees that the gulf in attitudes, perceptions and ultimately relations will widen rather than narrow between the two groups.

This has been tragically true in the sometimes scorching, even violent conflicts that have burst out between blacks and Latinos at some schools, in some neighborhoods and in California's jails and prisons. The conflicts there have been the subject of countless news articles, features and TV news stories, and prime the widely-held public perception that blacks and Latinos are hopelessly locked into a deadly cycle of warfare with each other.

CHAPTER 4

The Forbidden Zone

During his many years as Los Angeles County sheriff, Lee Baca has rarely come under fire from one of his bosses for his handling of affairs in the sheriff's department. But in February 2006, Baca was suddenly taking much heat from one of his superiors on the Los Angeles County Board of Supervisors. Supervisor Mike Antonovich, who had been one of Baca's staunchest supporters, was piqued at him for the latest in a string of bloody brawls that had shaken the Los Angeles County jails. The clashes were between blacks and Latinos in the jails and in the latest, a black inmate had been killed. Antonovich called the violence a "breakdown in management." Even more telling, Antonovich said that the sheriff should have done much more to safeguard the lives of blacks who were the prime targets of the attacks from alleged Latino gang members inside the jails. This was strong stuff coming from Antonovich, a conservative Republican. A chagrined Baca lashed back called it "an isolated incident," pleaded that he was doing everything possible to quell the violence, and urged the supervisors to put more money and resources into helping him restore order.

Though Baca drew fire and implicit blame for the inmate's death, bloody riots in America's jails and prisons are nothing new. In the past the battles between inmates were generally blamed on turf wars, renewal of gang rivalries, the ancient prison ritual of making a "rep" as a tough guy, and of course, black and white racial conflict. There was an ominous warning sign in 1982 that that could change. Thirty black and Puerto Rican inmates at Sumter Correctional Institution in Florida engaged in a bloody brawl. The clash perplexed prison officials. All one official could say was that the Hispanics "had some type of grievance with some of the blacks."

Order at the prison was quickly restored, and for the next decade, black and Hispanic inmates maintained an uneasy peace at most of America's jails. By the early 1990s, that had drastically changed. This time the violence rocked prisons and jails 2000 miles away in California. The Los Angeles County jails were the first to be wracked by deadly conflict in 1991.

And in the next few years, there were more than 150 racially motivated fights, mostly between black and Latino inmates in the jails. More than 80 inmates, most of whom were black, were injured in the violence, some seriously. The jail brawls became even more intense and bloody in 2005 and 2006 with more injuries and deaths. These weren't isolated racial assaults. Some Latino inmates deliberately attacked black inmates.

If some Latino inmates were systematically targeting black inmates solely because they were black, they had almost no chance of staying out of harm's way. The sprawling Los Angeles County jails are the biggest in the nation. More than 10,000 prisoners were housed at the four jails where the racial violence occurred. At these jails Latino inmates outnumbered black inmates more than 2 to 1. The massive warehousing of inmates, overcrowding, and agitation by groups such as the Mexican Mafia, who want greater control of California's prisons, have inflamed racial and ethnic tensions to a red-hot pitch.

Did the attacks stem solely from gang rivalries, prison turf battles, and feuds over drug sales? Authorities quickly pointed to all these as the main causes of the violence. The inescapable fact was that the victims in the beatings and killings were black or Latino, and there was much evidence that their color was the prime reason the violence was so bloody and prolonged.

The violence also seemed unique to California jails and

prisons. There was nothing comparable to it at prisons in Texas, Florida, New York and Illinois, where black and Latino inmates made up a majority or near-majority of the prisoners. New York City was probably the best example of how authorities took proactive action to head off black and Latino inmate violence.

In the mid 1990s, the jails in New York City were a tinderbox, as were California's jails and prisons, with inmate violence threatening to engulf them. Prison authorities moved quickly to head off trouble. They identified dozens of black and Latino gang leaders, implemented an intricate computer tracking system to identify the gang leader's movements, gang ID tags, their signs and language, and they dispersed them throughout the jail system. The system of tracking, dispersal, and tough sentencing for crimes committed inside the jails had repercussions outside the jails. When the Latin Kings, one of the top Latino gangs, reformed in New York's five boroughs, authorities were able to identify and isolate the leaders and made scores of arrests. Breaking the power of the gangs to foment violence and heighten racial tensions did much to reduce jail fears, as well as friction between black and Latino residents in neighborhoods where many of the inmates hailed from and that they would eventually go back to, with the added danger that they'd carry the same jail hatreds back to those neighborhoods.

The type of proactive action that New York jail officials

took to ward off ethnic clashes in New York's jails was not taken in California's prisons and jails, and prison officials made matters worse by segregating inmates by race. The policy was designed to control the violence by minimizing the physical contact between blacks and Latinos. The unintended consequence was that the forced separation increased the feeling of alienation, and deepened suspicions and antagonisms between the two groups, since prisoners now had little opportunity to interact in any kind of controlled setting.

Most of the young men involved in jail violence in California, as in New York City, ultimately would return to their neighborhoods. They could easily bring the same violence that they inflicted on each other behind bars back to those same neighborhoods.

· · · · ·

I t didn't take long for that to happen. There was no physical sign, barrier or even a chalk line that marked the zone where a black couldn't enter at the risk of grave harm. But the zone was there, and blacks knew that if they entered it they could be beaten, shot at or killed. The twist was that the forbidden line was not in a redneck, backwoods, Deep South town during the rigid and violent Jim Crow segregation era. The bigger twist was that the Klan, Neo-Nazis, racist skinheads and bikers didn't establish the racially restrictive zone. Purported Latino gang members established it. The forbidden zone was in a small, mixed ethnic bedroom community in the Harbor Gateway section of Los Angeles. The year was 2007, not 1947.

A black family that fled the community in 2006 in fear for their lives bluntly told a reporter that they left because blacks there were scared to death. In that year the hate terror escalated to the point where blacks told heart-breaking tales of being harried when they left their homes or when their children walked to school. They said that they were forbidden to go into a park and a convenience store.

This was not a bad case of racial paranoia run amok. Blacks were taunted, harassed, beaten and shot at in this community. But the tragic murder of Cheryl Green, a 14-year-old black girl, and the wounding of two other young blacks in the forbidden zone in one day of violence in December 2006 sparked anguish, rage and finally drew some local media attention. The murder drew gasps of disbelief that in America in 2007 in a big, cosmopolitan west coast city, with a Latino mayor, and that routinely back-patted itself for its ethnic diversity, there was an entire area that blacks were banned from on pain of injury or death at the hands of other non-whites. And city officials seemed powerless to do anything about it. Green wasn't the only black victim in the area. In a three-year span before Green was killed, Latinos had shot three other blacks.

Two reputed Latino gang members were charged with the teen's murder (ironically, one of them had a black parent) and were slapped with a hate crime charge. However, their arrest and the hate charge against them didn't calm the jitters and fears of blacks who lived in that neighborhood. Even after the arrests, a number of blacks still said that they planned to get out of the area as soon as they could.

• • • • •

Latino-on-black (and black-on-Latino) violence took two other appalling forms. The year before the attacks in Harbor Gateway, Latino men were robbed, beaten and even murdered in Plainfield, New Jersey, in Jacksonville, Florida, and in Annapolis, Maryland, and seven members of a Latino family were murdered in Indianapolis. The attackers in all cases were young black males. The men attacked were mostly undocumented workers, and police speculated that the attackers regarded them as easy prey for robbery since they would be reluctant to report the attacks to the police.

Was the motive for the attacks simply robbery? Or were they racially motivated as well? No matter what the motive, many Hispanics fervently believed that they were under siege from the blacks because they were Hispanic and immigrants. This reinforced the old racial stereotypes about blacks. A relative of one of those attacked in Jacksonville pulled no punches: "The vast majority of *morenos* (blacks) are hard workers, but the rest of them want to live for free." He painted blacks with the broad brush of stereotypes; that should be condemned. Yet it's hard for anyone to be objective when a loved one has been killed or injured when they perceive the attack to have been racially motivated.

Though the robberies, beatings and killings by blacks of Latinos in those cities were shocking, Los Angeles continued to dominate the headlines when it came to black and Latino violence. Four months before Green was murdered and a dozen miles from the Harbor Gateway neighborhood, five Latino members of the Avenues gang were convicted on federal hate crime charges and were slapped with life sentences. The U.S. Attorney tagged their crimes as a deadly effort to engage in "ethnic cleansing" during a four-year period that began in the late 1990s. The gang members launched their reign of terror to drive blacks out of the neighborhood. Two young blacks were killed in the violence.

In the next couple of years, according to Los Angeles police reports, there were more than a dozen murder attempts in other parts of Los Angeles by alleged Latino gang members on mostly young blacks that had had no known gang involvement in the latter part of 2006. A Los Angeles county Human Relations Commission report on hate violence in 2005 found that overall Latinos committed nearly half of the hate attacks in the County, while blacks committed thirty percent of the hate attacks. However, when it was Latino and black violence, the figure for hate violence soared. Latinos and blacks committed the bulk of the racially motivated hate attacks against each other. Nationally, blacks and Latinos commit about one in five hate crimes, and many of their victims, as in Los Angeles, are other blacks or Latinos.

This represents two more disturbing trends. One is that blacks and Latinos committed the majority of hate crimes in Los Angeles. The other is that hate crimes were increasingly being committed by blacks and Latinos against each other and that in some cases the victims such as Green were innocent random victims of the violence. The attacks have happened in mixed ethnic neighborhoods such as Harbor Gateway.

In the immediate preceding years before the Green killing, black and Latino hate violence against each other was rare. University of California, Irvine researchers found that of the 500 murders in South Los Angeles between 1999 and 2004, almost all of them were Latino-on-Latino, or black-on-black. Most residents in mixed black and Latino neighborhoods lived and got along in relative peace. But the increase in black and Latino hate crimes tragically showed that could be changing. That represents another colossal challenge to black and Latino leaders to find ways to stem the violence.

There are two easy explanations for the hate violence.

One is that the perpetrators are bored, restless, disaffected, jobless, untutored, or violence-prone gang members. Many appeared to match that profile. The other explanation is that the violence was a twisted response to racism and deprivation. The attacks no doubt were deliberately designed by the gang hate purveyors to send the message to blacks that "this is our turf, and you're an interloper." In Harbor Gateway, that hateful message was plainly stated as, "Don't let the blacks move in," reported former gang investigator Leo Duarte, an expert on the Mexican Mafia.

There is still another reason, though, more subtle and nuanced, as to why some gang members commit racial attacks. The violence is a source of ego gratification for them; negative stereotypes provided a convenient rationale for their violent acts. University researchers found that those individuals who suffer low self-esteem or have serious self-image problems are much more likely to view others, especially those they consider rivals, through the warped lens of racial stereotypes. That enhances their personal well-being, and makes it even more likely that they will continue to resort to negative typecasting as a self-image defense and boost. It is only a short step from that to rationalize, justify or even commit acts of violence against those they deem a threat, rival, or worse, an inferior.

Then there is the vehemence of the racial hate. The dirty and painful secret is that blacks and Latinos can be as racist toward each other as some whites can be toward them. It's easy to see why. Many Latinos continue to demean blacks for their poverty or type them as clowns, buffoons and crooks. Some routinely repeat the same vicious anti-black epithets as racist whites. A 1998 poll by the National Conference found that Latinos were three times more likely than whites to believe that blacks were incapable of getting ahead. These myths and stereotypes undergird the notion that blacks are a racial and competitive threat, and any distancing, ostracism, avoidance and even violence toward them seems a rational response to keep blacks at arm's length.

Again, stereotypes can cut two ways. Some blacks feed on the same myths and negative images of Latinos as anti-black, violence-prone gangsters who pose a menace, and who are their ethnic and economic competitors. The same 1998 poll found that as many blacks as whites believed that Latinos breed big families and that they are unable to support them. The warped misconceptions and fears of both groups have in many instances drowned out the repeated calls and efforts by black and Latino activists, and many residents in areas such as Harbor Gateway, to promote unity and peace in the neighborhoods that are torn by violence or where tensions have increased.

• • • • •

The murder of a black teen in Los Angeles in December 2006, and the gradual dawning that racially motivated hate attacks can happen right under the noses of a slumbering, possibly indifferent public and impotent city officials in a modern-day city like Los Angeles, did touch a mild nerve of disgust and ignite faint demands for action. Yet that wasn't nearly enough to erase the shame that for a brief time in America in 2007, there was a zone in a big city that blacks could only enter at mortal peril. And that zone wasn't marked by a burning cross or guarded by men in menacing white sheets and hoods.

No one could have predicted a few years ago the surge in black-on-Latino and Latino-on-black violence and worse, the surge in hate crimes in Los Angeles. The great danger was that Los Angeles's terrible implosion of brown-on-black hate violence and the attacks by blacks on Latinos in the other cities were bad signs. The challenge to Latino and black leaders was to make sure that L.A. was not the new, grim and ugly face of hate violence in America. That meant raising their voices whenever hate violence occurred in their neighborhoods.

Many residents did just that. A week after Green's murder, dozens of black and Latino residents showed their outrage at the attacks by staging a community rally for peace. Their rally was an important way of saying "no" to the violence.

CHAPTER 5

Reluctant Classroom Allies

Within days after becoming the first Hispanic mayor of Los Angeles in modern times in May 2005, an outwardly irritated Antonio Villaraigosa appeared at a meeting of the Los Angeles school board. He spared no words, "My sense frankly is that things are out of control at Jefferson. I do not get the sense that anyone is in charge." Then Villaraigosa virtually demanded that the principal of Jefferson High School in south Los Angeles step down. The mayor was incensed after three fights in three weeks between black and Latino students shook the school that was once predominantly African-American. The student clash briefly made national headlines. Villaraigosa's major concern was that order be restored at the school and that students, teachers and administrators work closely together to attain greater educational excellence.

His call for the ouster of the principal stirred some ill racial feelings. The principal under fire was African-American. Some blacks charged that he was being made the scapegoat for the violence that was increasingly being acted out between blacks and Latinos in the schools, and even more violently in the jails and on some city streets. That violence had resulted in injury and even the death of some blacks and Latinos.

A graphic arts instructor at the school, and an African-American, noted, "We have to understand that whoever is at the helm, it could happen to a new principal and it won't change what's going on." His quip was both an admonition and a warning that tensions between blacks and Latinos had become a cause for worry at some public schools. In the months immediately before the Jefferson High School clash, black and Latino students brawled at high schools in Reno, Nevada, in Monroe, Washington, as well as in Chicago, Oakland, Rialto, and San Jacinto, California.

The school clashes were blamed on overcrowding, inadequate resources, poor equipment, a shortage of textbooks, ill-trained and ill-prepared teachers, and a distant, unresponsive school bureaucracy. There were accusations from some blacks that school administrators and teachers gave preferential treatment to Latino students in some districts. There were also accusations by some Latinos that school personnel gave preferential treatment to blacks in other school districts.

· · · · ·

The conflict over which group of students was short-changed in education first surfaced in the battle over bilingual education in Washington, D.C. in 1995. Cooke Elementary School was located in a low-income, work-ing-class neighborhood that had once been predominantly black. The neighborhood was rapidly changing and there was a sharp jump in Central American immigrants. The school drew public attention when it garnered a $1 million federal grant. The money was to enhance bilingual instruction. That infuriated many black teachers and parents.

The black teachers feared that they would be trans-ferred or eased out of jobs completely if they couldn't speak Spanish. The parents demanded that the money be spent on textbooks, computers, and programs to enhance the overall quality of education. One black parent frankly said, " I don't want to see the nature of the school changed." The parent felt that spending on bilingual education would hurt black students.

Some politicians easily exploited the unease, and even hostility, on the part of many blacks toward greater spending and emphasis on bilingual education as a wedge issue. The potential for manipulation first surfaced in the "English only" drive in the early 1990s. It got a rocket boost in 1998 when businessman Ron Unz dumped millions into the campaign to pass Proposition 227 in California. The initiative's premise was simple. Bilingual education was costly, wasteful and ineffectual; non-English speaking students, mainly Hispanics, didn't learn much English in bilingual classes; and the programs were a sneaky way to promote multiculturalism.

The proposition drastically slashed funding for bilingual education programs. "English only" proponents boasted that students would learn English in a year or less if they simply spoke it. The proposition passed by a landslide. Blacks overwhelmingly backed the measure. They were among the most vehement in protesting that bilingual instruction hurt their children. "English only" quickly became the national rage.

In the next few years,"English only" groups popped up in dozens of states, and many blacks eagerly backed them. The groups subtly played on the dubious fear that multitudes of mostly poor, non-white, foreign-born immigrants were out to subvert English-speaking values and civilization. Voters and state legislators in 27 states bought the "English only" pitch, and enacted statues that specified English as the official language.

Four years after Proposition 227 ignited the "English

only" firestorm, educators took a closer look at the proposition to see if it had magically transformed non-English speaking students into proficient English speakers. They used language census figures from the California Department of Education. The results were dismal. Less than half of non-English speaking students enrolled in English immersion programs had attained proficiency in English. There was no tangible evidence that English immersion programs improved English skills of students faster or more effectively than bilingual education courses. Many parents demanded waivers to enroll their children in bilingual programs. By 2003, more than 100,000 students were taking bilingual classes.

Meanwhile, nearly a half million limited English speaking students were not "mainstreamed" into English programs. That meant they received no special help in learning English, and consequently their English language skills remained poor to non-existent.

The failure of the "English only" approach to create a generation of flawless English speaking students was no surprise. A decade earlier, a federal study to determine whether bilingual education helped or hindered the attainment of English proficiency concluded that bilingual education was not the losing proposition that "English only" advocates claimed. It found that well-funded and implemented programs enabled limited-English speaking students to catch up to their English-fluent students at a faster rate. It also found that it took students nearly five years to fully master English, and not the one year that "English only" backers claimed an immersion program would take.

The "English only" amendment nourished the racially tinged myth that immigrants don't want to learn English. In a speech to the National Federation of Republican Women in March 2007, one-time Republican House majority leader Newt Gingrich did much to further tinge the myth when he blurted that advocates of bilingual education in effect consigned Latinos to the language of the ghetto. The predictable furor was swift and noisy, and a chastened Gingrich quickly backpedaled, and profusely declared that he loved the Spanish language. Nonetheless, the damage had been done and the notion that bilingual education equals poverty and backwardness continued to dangle in the air.

It was a myth though. A nationwide survey in 2003 found that the great majority of Hispanics want bilingual education programs to focus exclusively on improving English language proficiency. The reason for that wasn't hard to figure. "Lack of English proficiency is the main cause for lower levels of education, "insisted Robert de Posada, president of the Latino Coalition that conducted the survey, "and for much of the discrimination Hispanics face."

• • • • •

Many black parents correctly continued to argue that cash-strapped school districts could hardly be expected to stem the astronomical dropout and illiteracy rates among black students without adequate funds, materials and trained staff. Many blacks, though, incorrectly continued to blame bilingual education for depriving their kids of the needed funds and teachers to improve the quality of their education. The complaining parents at Cooke and other schools were absolutely convinced that these programs were an unneeded and unwelcome drain on the budgets and resources of underserved schools in mostly black and poor neighborhoods.

At Cooke, many Latino parents sided with the blacks, and agreed that the funds should be used to improve the overall quality of education. They also contended that bilingual instruction was crucial to improving the reading and math proficiency skills for Spanish-speaking children. They felt that they couldn't advance educationally and professionally without these programs. The facts bore their contention out. The parents at Cooke were no different than many Latino parents at other poor, urban, and mostly segregated schools. Many Latino parents were less concerned than blacks in getting their kids into integrated schools than in getting more bilingual education programs. Latino leaders took the cue from the parent demands for more bilingual instruction and have been less aggressive in pushing for desegregation than blacks.

Many Latino groups, of course, have filed school desegregation lawsuits in decades past in California and Texas, and the landmark Brown school desegregation decision in 1954 was partly influenced by the massive lawsuit Mexican parents filed nine years earlier against several Orange County, California school districts. Then-NAACP chief counsel Thurgood Marshall always called that case the "dry run" for the Brown case. However, those immigrants who came to the U.S. in the 1990s and afterwards have been less willing to put the fight for school desegregation ahead of the fight for bilingual education as their priority.

The reason is not solely that they differ with the conservatives on the best path to English language proficiency experience. It's also a different experience with race and ethnicity than that of blacks. Though blacks are at the low end of the economic and social scale in Latin American countries and color is still very much the reason for that, racial discrimination was never as institutionalized in Puerto Rico, Mexico, Cuba and Central American countries as it was in the U.S. The feeling is not as intense among many Latino immigrants that their children are severely damaged by attending schools exclusively with other Latinos. Thus there's more of the sense that bilingual education programs are an absolute necessity for their children's advancement.

The obvious solution to the sharp difference in how both groups treat bilingual education and the fight for full school desegregation is to spend more on the educational needs of all students. However, when the money is not there, the problem quickly is reduced to ethnic infighting over the scarce education dollars. This sets off the torrid search for scapegoats for the abysmal failure of school districts to provide the badly needed dollars for school improvement and for perpetuating and even accelerating the number of poorly performing racially segregated schools that have multiplied since the mid-1990s.

· · · · ·

When the fight for educational excellence is wrongly transformed into an educational clash between blacks and Latinos for limited resources, it hurts minority students and shifts the burden of accountability to attain that excellence from teachers and school administrators. The failure of many districts to educate black and Latino students has become even more glaring as more and more of the nation's big city school districts are more racially segregated than a decade ago.

Beginning in the mid-1990s, Harvard University's Civil Rights Project warned in annual reports that many large urban school districts were becoming re-segregated and that there was a huge plunge in educational standards for the mostly black and Latino students in these schools. The project called many of these schools "apartheid schools" and noted that Latinos now top blacks in the number of students attending segregated schools in Texas and California, with a growing number attending segregated schools in New York, Chicago and Miami.

The students in these schools are poorer than students in predominantly or exclusively white schools. They do far worse in reading and math tests than non-black or black students at racially mixed schools. And for the first time studies in 2006 found that Latino students were dropping out in greater numbers than black students. The high dropout rates had devastating economic and social consequences for not only black and Latino communities but also American society in general. In California, as of 2005, the high dropout rate cost the state $14 billion in lost wages over the student's lifetimes, and added more than 1,000 inmates to state prisons, nearly all of whom were blacks and Latinos.

The black and Latino students who attend racially isolated schools are not in the schools because of Jim Crow segregationist laws, or failed school bussing policies. In fact, the two decades from the 1970s through the 1990s of pro-integration court decisions, limited bussing programs, civil rights legislation, and the election and the appointment of soaring numbers of blacks and Latinos to boards of education have racially remade public education. Black and Latino public school superintendents and top administrators are now fixtures in most urban school districts.

The persistence of housing discrimination and poverty, the near-universal refusal of federal and state courts to get involved in any more school desegregation cases, and the continuing flight of white (as well as black and Latino) middle-income persons to the suburbs have insured that even more poor black and Latino students would be perpetually trapped in segregated schools. The disconnected scattering of panaceas that President Bush, politicians and educators proposed to raise minority achievement levels since 2002 have included: school vouchers, fracturing urban districts, a wholesale dump of incompetent teachers and bureaucrats, magnet schools, and annual testing. Some districts advocate scrapping race altogether and using income and student interest as the criteria to achieve racially balanced schools.

However, these remedies help only a small number of black and Latino students. The bitter truth is that while segregated public schools are not the law of the land, they remain a fact of the land and the overwhelming majority of black and Latino students are stuck in them. Many of these schools, of course, are saddled with poor teachers, insensitive administrators, overcrowded classrooms, and shortages of books, learning materials and computers. The lack of uniform testing standards and the refusal of many school districts to hold teachers and administrators rigidly accountable for student performance are other prime causes of the educational stagnation in poor, majority-black and-Latino schools.

Then there's the endemic problem of funding. White middle-class suburban schools receive far more public money than poor, urban school districts. The federal government is the biggest offender in perpetuating the funding gap between rich and poor schools. In a study of school funding disparities in 2006, the Education Trust revealed that the wealthy school districts get a far bigger share of the $13 billion Title 1 funds that the government allocates supposedly to aid students from low-income families. In real dollars, a student in a wealthy school district gets nearly $1,000 more per year than a student in one of the highest poverty school districts. Most of those students in those districts are black and Latino.

• • • • •

These problems, as well as the continuing flight of white (and black and Latino) middle-income persons to the suburbs, guarantee that even more poor black and Latino students will be stuck in segregated schools for the immediate future. Yet, this is not a doom and gloom scenario where black and Latino students will be stuck in segregated, terribly under-performing schools in perpetuity and where they have to draw a line in the sand against other and squabble over resources, bilingual education or the pace of school desegregation. There are five crucial needs to attain educational excellence for black and Latino students and for their parents to avoid the rancor and fury they at times have aimed at each other.

The first need is to publicly acknowledge that the most segregated schools are urban school districts with a majority of black and Latino students. These districts should initiate an emergency program to upgrade the textbooks and facilities, purchase more computers, and place the highest caliber teachers, counselors and administrators possible at these schools. This also means that teachers' unions must actively work to enforce strict professional standards that hold teachers at these schools accountable for the performance of their students.

The second need is to bury the myth that black and Latino students in poorly performing schools can't or won't learn. Generations of black and Latino students attended mostly segregated schools in the South and the Southwest. Yet many managed to graduate, go on to college and become successful in business and the professions. Teachers who were dedicated and determined that they achieve in their studies taught them. These teachers expected and demanded that their students perform up to the same level as white students. They challenged the students to learn, set specific goals, demanded their full participation in classroom work, and gave them positive and continual direction and reinforcement. Many teachers and administrators at these schools also devised innovative learning methods that raised reading and math test scores and achievement levels.

The third need is for black and Latino educators, businesspersons and professionals to sponsor conferences in which they provide parents with learning tips and materials to help them improve the study habits of their children. They can also expand the economic and professional opportunities for poor students by creating and endowing programs that provide educational scholarships, career counseling, job and skills training programs, and computer training.

The fourth need is to understand that educational excellence can't be attained in segregated schools, or any school for that matter, unless parents do their part. This means they must attend parent-teacher conferences, monitor their children's classroom and homework assignments, join and get actively involved with the PTAs and parent-advisory councils at their local schools.

The final need is for black and Latino educators, parents and students not to battle over bilingual education spending, nor for Latino or black teachers and administrators to demand greater numbers of teachers and administrators from their own race. Restoring excellence at crumbling urban schools is the prime goal. To think that most, many or even all black and Latino students who attend segregated schools can't learn, master standard English or score high on performance tests is educational defeatism at best, and racial denigration at worst.

In 2003 black and Latino elected officials in Texas provided a positive, workable model for black and Latino cooperation to combat the educational neglect of black and Latino students. The Texas Legislative Black Caucus and the Texas Latino Education Coalition vigorously opposed a legislative education reform bill that cut funding for after-school initiatives, safe school programs, and library and technology funding. The black legislators did not object to a provision in the bill that slightly boosted spending on bilingual education programs. The black legislators and the Latino educators kept their focus solely on providing more resources and programs for the poorest and most under-performing schools. They did not pander to racial or ethnic politics.

They recognized that the funding gap between rich and poor districts, overcrowded classrooms, and substandard teachers and equipment wreaked profound damage on both black and Latino students. They got the funding hike and more quality education programs for black and Latino students. They showed that blacks and Latinos could be more than reluctant allies in the battle for classroom excellence: They can be full working partners in that battle.

It was doubly significant that politicians, in this case black politicians, were willing to join forces with Latino educators in the fight for decent schools. Now the question was: could black elected officials and Latino elected officials work harmoniously together on crisis issues that confront both groups given the surge in Latino voting numbers and the growing eagerness of Latino voters and politicians to flex their political muscle?

CHAPTER 6

Neither Political Friends nor Enemies

His Spanish was halting and stilted but it was Spanish nonetheless. And when President Bush in 2001 gave part of his weekly radio address to commemorate *Cinco de Mayo*, "In Texas, it's in the air you breathe. Hispanic life, Hispanic culture and Hispanic values are inseparable from the life of our state and have been for many generations." Bush's tribute to Hispanics in Spanish was a first for an American president. He promised that he would deliver at least part of his weekly addresses in Spanish in future broadcasts. The Democrats

in their own weekly radio address rolled out Texas Democrat Silvestre Reyes to deliver a rebuttal to Bush in Spanish.
Then House Minority Leader, Missouri Democrat Richard
Gephardt finished the address in English. It shouldn't have
surprised anyone if he and other House Democrats had
crammed in a Berlitz Spanish course, then tossed out a few
Spanish words in their future broadcasts.

The Spanish broadcasts by Bush and the Democrats
were not political grandstanding or a cheap bow to multi-
cultural correctness. In the 2002 mid-term national elections
Bush and the Democrats dumped millions of dollars into
campaigns to attract Latino voters to their respective party
banners. During the elections, Democrats enlisted Latino
Democratic politicians to exhort Latino voters to punch the
Democratic ticket. Republicans hoped that many Latino voters would stampede to the GOP mostly because of Bush. He
did more than any other Republican politician in recent years
to woo and win Latino voters in Texas. His praise of Mexico-
U.S. relations, support of the extension of the undocumented
immigrant registration deadline, and his broadcast in Spanish was a naked attempt to wash away the horrid taste past
Republican opposition to affirmative action and immigrant
rights had left in the mouths of many Latino voters.

During the 2004 presidential campaign, Bush raised the
stakes higher in the rush for Latino votes. Bush campaign officials announced with much public fanfare that they would sink

millions into ads on Spanish-language networks *Univision* and *Telemundo*. The first ads quickly hit the airwaves in New Mexico, Florida, Nevada and Arizona. The Democrats immediately said they'd match Bush dollar for dollar and would pour millions into campaign ads on Spanish-language TV.

The money Bush and the Democrats spent in 2004 on the TV ads far exceeded the money they had spent in past elections. In 1996, President Clinton spent a paltry $1 million on Spanish TV ads. Four years later Bush and the Republicans spent slightly more than $2 million on these ads. The campaign money spigot was now wide open. In the 2002 mid-term national elections, the Republicans and Democrats broke the spending record on Spanish language ads. They poured $9 million into 14,000 Spanish language spots on TV and radio. In 2004, the cash registers rang even louder: the total the Democrats and Republicans spent on Spanish language ads soared to $12 million.

The politicians didn't just pump money into ads and have party officials spout rote Spanish. They adroitly tailored their political pitches to their political Spanish-speaking audience. In Florida, there were Cuban-accented ads; in Texas, California and other Southwestern states, there were Mexican-accented ads.

• • • • •

The titanic shift in the nation's ethnic political landscape rudely shattered the myth that while Latinos convincingly outranked African-Americans as the nation's biggest minority group in 2004, they were still light years behind blacks politically. That argument might have had some plausibility as late as the 2000 election, when there were about 6 million Latino voters. Black voters numbered more than 2 and 1/2 times that figure. At that time, the Latino vote was still mostly regional and it was concentrated in California, Texas and other Southwestern states. The black vote in contrast was spread out nationally throughout the South, Midwest and Northeast. The other major impediments that still stymied the increase in Latino voting strength were age, language and the citizenship requirement. Latinos were younger, many still had not attained English language proficiency, and many were still not citizens. The result: less than 40 percent of Latinos were eligible to vote. For blacks the eligibility figure was 65 percent.

By 2004, three things began to change that. First, there was the continued jump in the Latino population, especially in the nation's big cities. How big, important and dramatic was that? In April 2007 the Census estimated that the population in New York, Boston and Los Angeles would have plunged by 2006 if the more than one million new immigrants hadn't swelled the numbers in these cities. The other two factors in the Latino political surge were an aggressive voter registration drive and citizenship preparation campaigns by Latino political and education groups, and pressure from Latino groups on the Justice Department to enforce provisions of the 1965 Voting Rights Act that prohibit language discrimination and restricted ballots. The Voting Rights Act was an especially powerful new weapon that Latino groups brandished. The complaints of discrimination from Latinos soared after the 2000 presidential election. They got action on those complaints. In Berks County, Pennsylvania, to take one example, Latino groups vehemently complained that Latinos were turned away from the polls because they couldn't read English fluently. The Justice Department ordered examiners to monitor county elections through June 2007 and to provide bilingual election materials and Spanish language interpreters for voters. This pleased Jonathan Encarnacion of Centro Hispano in Reading, Pennsylvania: "It was something that had to be brought to the surface." The population surge in the area guaranteed that. The Latino population had more than doubled in Reading between 1990 and 2000. Reading was no different than dozens of other counties throughout America where a decade earlier the Latino presence was barely a blip on the chart, and Latinos were reluctant to fight for their political rights. That was no longer the case.

The 8 million Latino voters in 2004 made up about eight percent of the vote nationally, and the numbers were steadily getting bigger. Three of America's biggest cities—San Antonio, Miami (for a decade), and Los Angeles—had Latino mayors. There were two Latinos in the Senate in 2004, and the Congressional Hispanic Caucus hit an historic high with two dozen members. Nationally, there were more than 5,000 Latino elected officials. The impressive rise in the number of Latino elected officials wasn't the only gauge of their surging political prowess. In the decade from 1991 to 2001, Latino growth in the number of legislative and government positions outstripped that of blacks.

It wasn't the numbers that excited Bush and worried the Democrats at the time, and caused some consternation among black elected officials. It was where those voters were concentrated and their political significance. The biggest numbers of Latino voters are in California, Florida, Texas and New York. These are the key electoral states that virtually determine who will sit in the White House. The consternation among blacks was that the expansion of Latino political strength beyond their traditional strongholds in Texas, California, New York and Florida and into states such as Illinois and New Jersey, which had seen a doubling and tripling of the number of Latino elected officials in 2004, would blunt black political strength. That didn't happen.

In 2006 Latino candidates and elected officeholders were competitive for state and federal offices in 38 states. In the eleven largest states, the Latino population grew four times faster than that of blacks. The Latino population surge was even greater in Pennsylvania, Georgia, Florida and Texas. At one time it was thought blacks in these states would likely gain more members of Congress. Suddenly, the prospect was great that more gains in Congressional offices in those states would be made by Latinos, not blacks: "This widespread competitiveness reveals the growing Latino political maturity," insisted Arturo Vargas, Executive Director of the National Association of Latino Elected Officials Educational Fund. For Vargas the numbers and the national reach of Latino voters also showed that they could raise money, get key endorsements and mount voter registration drives to get even more Latinos registered.

The use of Latino population numbers, the emphasis on bloc voting, and Latino economic power, by Latino politicians to showcase the importance of the Latino vote to Republicans and Democrats was not a novel approach to wresting greater political concessions from the two parties by an ascending ethnic group. Latinos were duplicating the model that blacks had used for decades to boost the number of black voters and to gain influence within the Democratic Party, and by 2000, the Republican Party. The NAACP, the Congressional Black Caucus and the Southern Christian Leadership Conference had repeatedly launched voter education and registration drives, and demanded funds and endorsements from top white Democrats for black candidates.

• • • • •

Now that Latinos had become potentially powerful new political players, Republican strategists figured that if they could ramp up their share of the Latino vote by as little as five percent, they would top the Democrats in Arizona, Nevada, New Mexico and Florida in the 2000 and 2004 elections and possibly in future national elections. In the 2000 presidential election, presidential candidates Al Gore and George Bush traded razor-thin victories in those states. *The National Survey of Latinos: The Latino Electorate,* conducted in 2002 by the Pew Hispanic Center, found that one-fifth of Latinos were Republicans.

It also confirmed the not-so-subtle link between race and party affiliation. The overwhelming majority of the Latinos who self-identified as Republicans also self-identified as "white." That corresponded with the Pew survey which found that those most likely to be Republican were wealthier, better educated, and at least in their racial eyes, white.

The Republican outreach campaign worked well in 2004. Bush got more Latino votes than any other Republican president in history (roughly forty percent).

His anti-gay marriage, anti-abortion, and family values plug resonated with a significant number of the more than 20 million Hispanic evangelicals in America. By contrast, the much less ambitious Republican outreach among blacks did not come close to making the same gains. Though Bush bumped his vote total among blacks in Florida and Ohio, he still sunk to single digit figures among black voters in most states. Black voters still intensely feared and loathed both him and his policies.

The more optimistic among Republicans in 2004 talked about giving the Democrats a real run for the Latino vote in California. Though the majority of Latinos in past elections in California had voted in big numbers for the Democrats, there appeared to be some chinks in the Democrats' armor in 2004. During the 2003 recall election against Democratic Governor Gray Davis, Republican Arnold Schwarzenegger garnered more than one-quarter of the Latino vote. The Latinos who backed him rejected the Democrats' political gambit to give illegal immigrants driver's licenses. Polls showed that many Latinos opposed the measure, and also said more should be done to control illegal immigration. The Republicans believed that they could use Schwarzenegger's popularity with many Latinos to help Republicans.

The strategy worked to some extent for Schwarzenegger in his landslide re-election win for governor in 2006 only because he reversed gears, distanced himself from conservative Republicans on liberal immigration reform, and convinced Latinos that he would be immigration reform-friendly in the future. While the immigration issue proved a winner for Schwarzenegger, it meant little to black voters in California who remained ambivalent or indifferent about it. The overwhelming majority of them still supported his Democratic opponent.

In the world of politics there are always winners and losers, sometimes big winners and losers, and that was just as true
in the world of ethnic politics. The dash by Republicans and
Democrats to court Latino voters touched off nervous jitters
among some black politicians and leaders. If Latinos were now
not only the favored minority of record, but also the favored
minority political group of record, blacks would be shoved
even further onto the backburner of American politics.

During the 2004 Democratic presidential primaries,
they murmured loud in the early days of the contests that the
seven white male Democratic presidential contenders were
virtually mute on miserably failing inner city schools, soaring black unemployment, prison incarceration and the HIV/
AIDS crisis that has torn apart black communities.

The Democrats continued to draw heavy fire from blacks
for their perceived penchant to take the black vote for granted.
This was more than blacks expressing personal antagonism at
being snubbed by politicians. Blacks were slowly losing political ground. They had lost dozens of mayoralties and municipal offices and had garnered fewer political appointments in
cities across the country. Since 2000, the rise in the number
of black elected officials nationally, especially male elected officials, has slowed to a crawl. What growth there has been
has come almost exclusively among black females. The largest
number of black elected officials remained concentrated in a
handful of Deep South states and Illinois.

The mild fall-off in black political power for a time was glaring in California, the biggest and most politically significant state. From 1996 to 2006, the number of blacks in the state legislature had been cut in half. Though blacks made some resurgence in the number of new members in the legislature in 2006, the number of Latinos in state government continued to speed forward. They hold a sizeable number of seats in the state legislature and some of the most visible positions in state government, including the Lieutenant Governor post.

Part of the blame for the black political malaise lay not with the run-up in the number of Latino voters and their spiraling political clout but with the failure of many black politicians to excite black voters on the issues. They have tied their string so tightly to the Democratic Party that they make it easy for the Democrats to take their vote for granted. This has created apathy, indifference and cynicism among black voters who feel that many black political leaders have betrayed their political interests. Many black Democrats will not expend great time and energy to pressure the Democrats, let alone the Republicans, to take them and their agenda seriously.

Many black politicians and voters, in their blindness to the rapidly changing Latino political reality nationally, have failed to forge coalitions with other ethnics, while continuing to swear unwavering allegiance to the Democrats.

Many Latino leaders and elected officials and voters aren't hamstrung by this self-defeating burden. In California and Texas there were politically active and influential Latino Republican legislative caucuses in 2002 and afterwards. Latinos are willing to parcel out more of their votes to the Republicans. This political diversity and flexibility was much in evidence in 2003 to the great chagrin of Latino and black Democrats when a handful of Latino Republican congresspersons formed the Congressional Hispanic Conference. They were unabashed Bush backers.

In their mission statement, they boasted that they unequivocally backed Bush's war on terrorism, the Iraq war, free trade, school vouchers, and the faith-based initiative. A similar tout of any aspect of Bush's agenda would have been unthinkable for black Democrats, and since there were no black Republicans in Congress, the Congressional Hispanic Conference stuck out as a group of political mavericks. "Many Americans think the Congressional Hispanic Caucus represents Hispanics, noted Texas Republican Representative Henry Bonilla in announcing the formation of the Conference. "It's the arm of the extreme left of the Democratic Party, the attack dog of the left." So now the Republicans had their Hispanic attack dogs, and the Conference would take every opportunity it got to nip at the Democrats, especially Hispanic Democrats.

The expanding Latino presence in Congress and the Republican Party and the sizeable Republican Latino vote forced Bush to take a much softer approach than conservatives wanted in his Supreme Court brief against the University of Michigan's race-based affirmative action program in 2005, and prompted him to throw his political weight behind lobbying for a moderate immigration reform bill and to oppose the "English only" amendments and resolutions that cropped up in Congress.

· · · · ·

I n the future to be competitive politically, any black political aspirant in majority Latino districts (or districts that are approaching a majority in California or other states) will have to work harder and smarter to convince Latino voters that they can deliver the goods for them at City Hall and in state legislatures. Those who can't will have no hope of being a political factor.

One black politician who quickly realized that the path to political power lay in convincing Latino voters that he could deliver the political goods was Ron Dellums. The veteran and politically savvy former California congressman came out of retirement in 2006 to vie for the mayor's job in Oakland. Dellums was the handpicked choice of the old guard in Oakland black politics. They were alarmed at the prospect that blacks would lose political power in the city to Latinos. Blacks had a majority on the city council and black mayors had run city hall for most of the past three decades. That could suddenly change. Before Dellums entered the race, Oakland City Council president Ignacio De La Fuente was the odds-on favorite to win the mayor's contest. Fuente was an immigrant from Mexico and represented a mostly Latino district in Oakland. He was a proven vote getter. It was hoped that Dellums could beat back the challenge from Fuente.

Dellums, though, had other ideas about the campaign. He did not play the ethnic card. He stuck to the issues of creating more jobs, attracting more business, beefing up public safety, and providing more affordable housing that appealed to Latino and black voters. Fuente did the same and did not attempt to make the race a contest between blacks and browns for political power. As expected, Dellums got solid support from black voters. But he also pitched hard to Latino voters and got a significant number of their votes in his win.

He was politically mature and shrewd enough to build a black and brown alliance on common big-city issues and problems without expressly calling it an alliance. Political analyst Robert Smith, who closely observed the Oakland mayoral race, noted about Fuente and Dellums, "They've gone beyond making ethnicity a big issue. They have to build a multiethnic coalition. That's the only way to win and the only way to govern." Dellums and Fuente proved that ethnic rivalry and discord did not have to taint a contest to win power at city hall in cities where blacks and Latinos increasingly were the majority.

Dellums' subtle multiethnic approach was the key to

winning city hall. Even so, black politicians in some cases will have to face another political fact. Many Latinos have gotten their first real taste of political power with their growing vote numbers in some urban areas that are transitioning to majority Latino districts. They will want to elect a Latino to office in those districts. That's no different than what other emerging ethnic groups such as the Irish, Italians, Poles and Jews have done in big cities during the years between World Wars I and II when they began to have the numbers and the resources to elect one of their own to office. Blacks followed the same political path to power. In the 1970s they made a wholesale rush to elect blacks as large city mayors, to city councils, state assemblies and Congress solely based on race.

Ethnic loyalty and pride more often than not blinded blacks to the lack of qualifications and competence of some candidates when it came to voting. It took two decades for many black voters to gain the political maturity to inch past electing a black solely because they were black. Many Latino voters will and are going through the same political growing pains. But even as they go through their political growth phase, many Latino voters showed in the mayoral races in Houston and Oakland that they would back a black candidate for office if they felt he or she would fight for their concerns.

• • • • •

Still, a core of Latino Democrats have not made the mistake that some black Democrats made in the past in tying their political string too tightly to the Democratic Party and gaining no political favors in return. They have warned top Democrats that they tread with great peril if they take the Latino vote for granted. In the wake of the defeat of Democratic presidential contender John Kerry in November 2004, thirty Latino Democrats huddled in Washington, D.C. to map out a political strategy to derail Bush's efforts to boost Latino voter support for the GOP and to pressure top Democrats to place greater emphasis on Latino interests. Party officials jumped at the plan and formed the Coronado Project.

The Latino Democrats then sent a memo to Democratic Party officials and sternly admonished that failure to court Latino voters would be "suicidal." They demanded that the party spend millions more on voter registration campaigns and ads, promote Hispanic candidates and make immigration reform a cornerstone of Democratic Party policy.

The Democrats got the message and vowed to ramp up their spending and outreach to Latinos in the 2006 mid-term national elections, and even more in the 2008 presidential contest. They had no choice but to heed the warning, especially since the immigrant rights groups had shown that they could put hundreds of thousands in the streets. Those thousands could be translated into votes, and if there is one thing politicians have always been keenly adept at, it is counting votes.

The DJs on Spanish language radio stations who played a huge role in getting those thousands in the streets made doubly sure that Democrats and Republicans got the message. They implored the marchers to become citizens. The chant in the streets became, "Today we march, tomorrow we vote." At a giant rally in downtown Los Angeles in March 2006, one protestor observed, "The only way anyone will listen to us is if we vote." The words were simple and heartfelt, and they neatly summed up the changing state and face of ethnic politics in America.

Yet the nagging question that still dangled in the air was whether black and Latino voters and elected officials would do more than pay lip service to building coalitions to increase the political clout of both groups. One test of that was the ongoing jockeying for political power by both groups in and outside of the city halls in America's big cities.

CHAPTER 7

Black and Brown Political Coalitions: Fact or Romantic Image

The Reverend Norman S. Johnson was a lonely man in the spring of 2001. The then-executive director of the Southern Christian Leadership Conference–West was one of only two of the city's more influential black leaders to endorse Los Angeles mayoral candidate Antonio Villaraigosa. Nearly every other prominent black leader and black elected official had endorsed Villariagosa's white opponent, Los Angeles city attorney James Hahn. Villaraigosa knew that black voters were wary and suspicious of him. He was determined to try to do whatever he could to reassure them that if he won, it would not mean (as some blacks openly said) that Mexicans would now run city hall. Villaraigosa barnstormed through Los Angeles, promising to forge a multiethnic coalition that would be a model for racial peace and progress in Los Angeles and the nation. Villaraigosa was the right man to try to forge such a coalition. He was a former civil rights and labor activist and a self-described progressive Democrat. He could also make history by being the first Latino mayor in this century of America's second biggest city.

Villaraigosa got strong support from Latinos, Asians and Jews, and that support propelled him to a surprising first place finish in that year's primary over the favorite, then Los Angeles city attorney, James Hahn, a white centrist Democrat. The two candidates faced off in the June 2001 general election.

His primary election success seemed to prove that his multi-ethnic pitch worked. He was the odds-on favorite to beat Hahn. Despite predictions of an easy victory and that he would make political history for Latinos, Hahn overwhelmed him in the general election. Political pundits scratched their heads, and asking themselves what they might have missed.

The miss could be summed up in three words: the black vote. The bitter reality was that Villaraigosa's approach crashed on deaf ears with black voters. He got less than one-fifth of the black vote. They made up nearly one out of five Los Angeles voters. They gave Hahn a phenomenal 80 percent of their vote. That was the decisive factor that powered him to victory.

Political observers assumed that Hahn, and not Villaraigosa, got the majority of the black vote because blacks had fond memories of his father, Kenny Hahn, who had served as a Los Angeles County supervisor for nearly four decades and was a stout civil rights fighter. This was the politically correct explanation. There was certainly much nostalgia among many blacks for the past, and they made a hardheaded calculation that Kenneth's son, James would fill the giant shoes of his father and be a champion of black interests. The much less charitable politically incorrect explanation was that black voters in Los Angeles were wary, even fearful and hostile, toward Latinos and would oppose Villaraigosa in big numbers.

He was not unaware of the political fear and hostility of many blacks toward him; he had learned that from bad experience. In 2004, he aggressively feted black community groups, church leaders and activists, showed up at numerous black community meetings, rallies, events, and functions, and hammered on the pulsating theme that he'd be mayor of all the people. He promised that if elected, his administration would be racially inclusive. He even wrapped himself in the mantle of Tom Bradley. Bradley had been the city's first black mayor and had won five terms based on the artful building of strong coalitions with the city's patchwork quilt of ethnic groups. This time around the coalition model worked for Villaraigosa. He got the endorsement of many black elected officials who had spurned him four years earlier.

When he took office in July 2005, Villaraigosa was suddenly hailed as the Latino politician who was most adept at building coalitions, especially with blacks. On election night, every top Democrat from Democratic National Committee Chairman Howard Dean to Bill and Hillary Clinton were on the phone to him, cooing, courting and praising him as the Democratic Party's new political darling. But there were two problems, and the problems pointed to the unsettling difficulties in crafting a sustained black and Latino political alliance.

· · · · ·

Marcelo Gaete, an analyst with the National Association of Latino Elected and Appointed Officials, pointed to the first problem. She noted that the ability to put together coalitions across ethnic lines is the key to political success in building Latino political power: "Part of the story of the growing Hispanic political clout is Hispanic's (people's) demonstrated ability to put coalitions together nationally." The Senate victories of Ken Salazar in Colorado and Mel Martinez in Florida in 2004 on the surface seemed to bear that out. But both were seasoned politicians, and they made no special appeals to Latinos.

More blacks bought Villaraigosa's multiethnic pledge in the 2005 election than four years before. Yet there was less in his win than met the eye. Hahn was a lackluster bureaucrat, tainted by an ethics scandal and reviled by many blacks for firing the popular black Los Angeles Police Department chief Bernard Parks. He also did little outreach to blacks. However, despite his slippage in popularity, Hahn still got more black votes than Villaraigosa got in the primary election in March 2005.

Villaraigosa's forceful court of black voters and his refusal to make special appeals to Latino voters was the second difficulty in building effective political alliances between blacks and Latinos. Some Latinos complained that he might not be as forthright in promoting Latino interests. That was a false fear. He did not have to do any special outreach to Latinos. They were more than forty percent of the population in Los Angeles in 2005 and comprised more than 30 percent of the city's voters.

Their presence as a dynamic new force in city politics by then had become evident. Yet in the first flush of his victory, that was sufficient reason to heighten the expectations of some Latino activists that he'd do more to boost Latino interests. That expectation, coupled with the fragility of his black political support, raised doubts about how deep and lasting his multiethnic alliance really could go. Columbia University political scientist, Rodolfo De La Garza, openly scoffed at the belief that he had cobbled together a solid black-Latino political coalition, calling it "a romantic image."

• • • • •

Villaraigosa's winning black and brown alliance may have been a romantic image, but it sent a shot across the bow to black politicians in Los Angeles that their days of power sharing at city hall could be nearing an end. In 2006, they still had thirty years of unbroken political power in representing three south Los Angeles districts. But the ethnic demographics in their districts had changed. Immediately after the 1992 Los Angeles riots when national leaders talked about south Los Angeles, they assumed that these neighborhoods were exclusively black. Even then there were signs that that was changing. Latinos then made up about one third of the area's residents. In 2006 they were a statistical majority in the three formerly predominantly-black districts of south Los Angeles.

The three councilpersons who represented the districts as of 2007 cling precariously to their political power only because the majority of the Latinos in their districts are either non-citizens or their school- aged children are too young to vote.

In time that will also change. In 2004 there were more than two million Latino voters in California. By 2010 they will makeup about forty percent of the state's voters. In Los Angeles County, the percentage of Latino voters will be much higher. The estimate is that in less than a decade Latinos will comprise one out of three voters, and that may be a gross undercount.

In the three south Los Angeles council districts, their numbers will grow even faster than that, due to the availability of cheap housing and access to lower-end manufacturing and retail industry jobs in the area. In addition, more Latino immigrants will become citizens, their children will become eligible to vote, and relentless voter registration drives by Latino political groups for the 2008 presidential election will soon translate their numerical majority into a major jump in their vote percentage in the districts.

Yet, long before that happens, the city's term limits rule (councilpersons are restricted to three four-year terms) could accelerate the pace for Latino candidates to contest their seats, since the black councilpersons could be forced out of office. The black candidates in turn who try to fill their shoes will not have the money, experience, city hall clout or name identification to guarantee that the district's core black voters will reflexively vote for them.

The possibility looms that blacks will lose one, possibly two, and, in a worst-case scenario, all three seats they currently hold on the Los Angeles City Council. And it's that possibility that sends shivers up the political spines of all other aspiring black politicians and leaders in Los Angeles. When the city's black political meltdown eventually happens, the three black congresspersons who represent South Los Angeles districts could face the same bleak rules of political disengagement as the black city councilmembers and state legislators. Latinos makeup the statistical majority in their districts and will soon be the voting majority. While the black congresspersons can't be termed out, they can be voted out, and if they don't deliver the goods to their majority-Latino constituents, they could be dumped from office. California Assemblyman Mervyn Dymally, a former congressman from one of those districts, recognized that change can and probably will come: "There are no safe African-American districts anymore."

Blacks and Latinos got a foretaste of that in the city that's neighbor to Los Angeles when Latinos elected a majority Latino city council in Lynwood, California in 1997. Before that the city had had a black majority on the council and a black mayor. Many blacks girded themselves for the worst. Some Latinos openly gloated and swore that they would not share power with blacks, and it appeared that they had made good their threat when the city fired several black employees and severed business ties with some black contractors. There were reported discrimination lawsuits and settlements as a result of the action. But it also triggered a soul search on the part of many blacks and Latinos about power sharing, what that meant and how to attain it.

In 2003 Lynwood took a step toward burying some of the past ethnic rancor when city councilperson Leticia Vasquez assumed the mayor's spot. Though she said that she still took some heat from Mexican-Americans about what they regarded as her too-close ties with blacks, especially black elected officials, she made a determined effort to build bridges between blacks and Latinos in the city. She didn't call it coalition politics but that's what it amounted to, and that did much to ease the fears of blacks that Latinos in the city targeted them for political annihilation.

Los Angeles's fast-changing ethnic picture is the first snapshot of the change that inevitably will come in other big cities across the country with neighborhoods that are transitioning from black to Latino or where Latinos are a significant and growing percentage of that district's voters.

· · · · ·

Villaraigosa's apparent success in getting blacks to vote for a Latino candidate did not go unnoticed by some black and Latino elected officials in other cities. In New York, Bronx Borough President Fernando Ferrer announced that he'd run again for mayor in 2005. In Chicago popular Congressman Luis Gutierrez eyed a mayoral bid in 2007. Both had substantial backing from Puerto Rican voters, but that wouldn't be nearly enough to put them over the top in a tough mayor's race against popular and seasoned incumbents. They'd need the black vote.

Blacks make up a much bigger share of the vote in those cities than in Los Angeles, are much more politically cohesive, and for decades have been an entrenched force in politics in the two cities. Ferrer, like Villaraigosa, realized that much hinged on how well blacks responded to his plea for support. Ferrer lost in the Democratic primary in 2001 where he got more than 70 percent of the Latino vote but failed to get the endorsement of key black politicians, and that included former New York City mayor David Dinkins. His white opponent in the Democratic primary, Mark Green, got more than 40 percent of the black vote.

It was an uphill battle again for him in 2005. This time he faced Michael Bloomberg, the incumbent, a wealthy, well-connected colorless moderate. Ferrer had mixed success with black voters. He got nearly half their vote, but a huge number of blacks also backed Bloomberg. That spelled a prime difference in the race. Ferrer simply didn't excite or energize blacks enough to make them sprint to the polls in big enough numbers to give him an edge.

Gutierrez ultimately decided not to run for mayor in

2007. He correctly figured that five-term mayor Richard Daley was unbeatable even if he managed to get substantial black support, which in itself was highly problematic.

City politics was not the only model for fruitful black and Latino political cooperation. The critical issues of affirmative action, affordable health care, job expansion, prison reform, the 1965 Voting Rights Act extension and the Iraq war were still compelling issues that impacted hard on both poor and working class blacks and Latinos. These were the issues on which the Congressional Hispanic Caucus and the Congressional Black Caucus repeatedly and publicly vowed to work together. They made real efforts to do that. The NAACP was so pleased with the effort at unity that it gave CHC chairman California Democrat Joe Baca an "A" rating on its legislative report card, and gave high marks to other members of the caucus. In a press statement, a glowing Baca thanked the NAACP for recognizing "my work to advance equal rights for all Americans."

Villaraigosa's victory in Los Angeles, Ferrer's valiant effort in New York to get black support, and the cordial legislative working relationship between the CBC and the CHC all comprised the first stop, on what one Latino politician called a "map of the future." But it was only the first stop and just how far blacks and Latinos would travel on that political map depended on whether Villaraigosa's administration would be truly inclusive of blacks, and whether other Latino candidates and incumbents would follow his lead and balance-out the demands for inclusion from blacks and pressure from some Latinos to be the "Latino candidate or incumbent."

That pressure would certainly be on them. "The key to continued expansion of Hispanic political power, observed political scientist Christine Sierra, "will be how they respond to the Hispanic support that got them into office and reach beyond that." That was the crucial and still-unanswered question that only time would answer. The future of whether blacks and browns could form viable and sustained political coalitions hinged heavily on the answer.

The one problem that loomed as a big obstacle to black and Latino relations, and defied an easy answer, was immigration. In the early months of 2006 the issue exploded into a fierce national debate between pro-and anti-immigration reform forces. The debate forced many blacks to choose sides. It wasn't the first time in the history of the immigration wars that blacks had to choose sides.

CHAPTER 8

Immigration an Age-Old Black Fear

"Every hour sees the black man elbowed out of employment by some newly arrived emigrant." A century and a half ago, as early as the 1850s, a conflicted Frederick Douglass saw immigration as a looming threat to the fragile and piecemeal economic gains that northern blacks had made in some trades and industries. The famed black abolitionist and pioneer civil rights champion was no lone voice in denouncing immigration. During the half century from the formal end of slavery in 1865 to the immediate post-World War I years, black leaders waged ferocious fights with each other over ideology, politics and leadership, but they relentlessly opposed immigration. "The continual stream of well-trained European laborers flowing into the West," warned educator Booker T. Washington in an 1882 speech,"leaves Negroes no foothold."

Washington's great concern was that immigration would displace Northern blacks from manufacturing industries, and that Southern landowners would use cheap European and Asian labor to boot blacks off the land. Educator and civil rights activist W.E.B. DuBois bitterly opposed Washington's racially conciliatory views. Yet, like Washington, he attacked immigration as a dire threat to blacks. He accused "the northern industrialist of the promotion of alien immigration to eliminate black workers and depress wages."

During and immediately following World War I, millions more eastern and southern Europeans poured into the country to escape war, poverty, hunger and anti-Semitic pogroms in Russia and Poland. Many were poorly educated, marginally skilled workers who crowded the cities and muscled blacks out of the ground level manufacturing and farm jobs. America first immigration foes, as well as black leaders and rabid racists from the rest of society, screamed loudly for Congress to stop the flood of new immigrants.

In an editorial in 1919, the *New York Age* skipped the niceties: "Speaking purely from a motive of self-interest, the

American Negro can say that the passing of a law restricting immigration for four years is a good thing." Two years later the *Chicago Defender*, which had virtually become the bible for black America readers by the early 1920s, chimed in: "The restrictions recently placed upon immigration to these shores ought to help us if they do not help anybody else." In a speech in 1920, black nationalist Marcus Garvey (himself an immigrant from Jamaica) painted an even scarier picture of what unchecked immigration could mean for blacks: "We will be out of jobs, and we will be starving." It was vintage over-the-top-stir-the- masses Garvey rhetoric. But it tapped a nerve in some blacks.

The racist, eugenicist theories propounded by Madison Grant in his 1916 book *The Passing of the Great Race,* an unabashed tout of white (Nordic) supremacy when heavily influenced Congress when it passed the blatantly racially exclusionary anti-immigration act in 1924. Yet much of the black press cheered madly at its passage.

The radical, pro-socialist, pro labor *Messenger* instantly hailed the bill as a victory for black workers, and claimed that it would open up more jobs. A year later, the National Urban League's house organ *Opportunity* which championed black professional and business interests and relentlessly opposed the *Messenger's* pro-socialist views, still applauded the anti-immigrant assault: "The gaps made by the reduction in immigrant labor have forced a demand for Negro labor despite theories which hold that they are neither needed nor desired."

• • • • •

The flutter among many blacks around the idea that immigrants threatened to undermine the marginal gains blacks had made in Northern industries was not merely an early 20th century case of blacks pandering to the prevailing paranoia of that era over the alleged immigrant peril. Blacks accurately perceived that immigrants had a built-in advantage over them. They were white and European, or at least non-black, and they did not have the same intense racial stigma that burdened blacks, nor were they subject to Jim Crow segregation laws, racially restrictive covenants on homes, and banned from most neighborhoods, routinely denied business and home loans, nor threatened with racial violence solely because of their color.

The brutal color bar against blacks created a rigid racial hierarchy in society and stymied black job gains in industries. Employers in the auto, steel and garment manufacturing industries made no secret that they preferred immigrant labor to blacks. Many immigrants were more than willing to take the jobs, and in some cases engage in violence against blacks to keep them out of low-skilled or unskilled jobs where competition with black workers was the most intense.

The blunt truth was that a racial pecking order put whites or non-blacks above blacks on America's economic ladder and gave immigrants, especially white European immigrants, a colossal boost in America. That point has been made repeatedly when discussing the glaring differences between the experiences of waves of European immigrants and the waves of blacks who migrated from the South to the cities in the years immediately before and after World War I. "Blacks have been used as psychological, cultural and economic stepping-stones for the social and economic advancement of new groups," declared sociologist Stanley Leiberson.

In an even more bitter twist on the immigrant experience versus that of blacks, the immigrants may have been ridiculed, demeaned, impoverished, subject to religious persecution and repression and violence in the countries they had come from, and that especially included the violence against the Jews in Russia and Eastern Europe. For a time they suffered cultural slights and discrimination in the United States, but that was temporary.

For blacks it persisted for decades, both in custom and law, and for poor blacks has persisted even to the present. "Despite being victims of oppression themselves, they soon came to share with other white Americans the conviction that blacks were not the equal of any white," notes sociologist Benjamin Ringer, "and were therefore not entitled to the same rights and immunities as whites."

Nonetheless, it was an inflated exaggeration to fully blame immigrants for the loss of black jobs. If not one European immigrant had ever set foot off the boat at Ellis Island in New York, or no Latino immigrant had ever waded across the Rio Grande from Mexico, or no Chinese immigrant had been herded off a cattle boat in San Francisco during the years from 1900 to the end of World War I, blacks would still have been subjected to raw racial violence, iron clad segregation laws, urban poverty, Southern peonage and the stigma of inferiority.

That would have made them labor expendables. And where they worked, they would still have been relegated to the lowliest, dirtiest and marginal-subsistence jobs, the doors would have still been slammed shut to them in corporations and in many of the professions, and most unions would have still kept their "whites only" clauses firmly in place.

• • • • •

The 1924 restrictive immigration law didn't totally allay black dread that immigration would unhinge their tenuous economic plight. In fact, they now had a new group—Hispanics—that some believed posed the same grave threat as the European immigrants to their shaky spot on the low end of America's racial and economic hierarchy. The cruel irony was that the 1924 Act which was openly labeled the Asian Exclusion Act, or National Origins Act, was aimed at barring Asians and drastically reducing the number of southern European immigrants. It placed no limits on immigrants from Latin America. Presumably that meant Mexican immigrants as well. Still, black newspapers gave the first dire warning in the 1920s that Mexican immigrants could push blacks out of jobs. In 1927 the *Pittsburgh Courier* pushed the panic button and claimed that Mexican immigrants would "menace" blacks' position in industry: "The Mexicans are being used as laborers on the railroads, on public works and on the farms, thus taking the places of many Negro workers." The *Courier* did not blame Mexican immigrants for taking jobs, but regarded them as pathetic pawns of greedy, unscrupulous employers to depress wages and labor standards and to sow divisions with black workers.

Though the *Courier* bitterly criticized employers for exploiting illegal immigrants, it did not take the next step and urge black workers, labor groups and civil rights leaders to join with Mexican workers and fight for better wages, fair hiring practices and improved labor standards, and against Jim Crow segregation that impoverished both black and Mexican workers. This was the pre-Depression era of naked, *laissez faire* capitalism, and the black press and black leaders banked on the goodwill of white corporate employers for the meager and menial jobs they were allowed to work. It was also a question of numbers.

The *Courier* wailed that Mexican immigrants would snatch jobs from blacks in public works and railroads in the 1920s. But the estimated half million or so Mexican illegal immigrants that trickled into the U.S. then were a relatively low number. They were mostly concentrated in the Southwest and posed no direct threat to blacks in the industrial North. Still, in singling out Mexican illegal immigration as a potential danger to blacks in the 1920s, the *Courier* gave verbal ammunition to opponents of illegal immigrants that blacks decades later would eagerly pick up and fire at them.

A century ago, at the end of the 19th and in the first years of the 20th century, Douglass, Washington, DuBois, Garvey and the black press sounded the alarm bell over legal and illegal immigration. They forged a strange alliance with conservative and even peripheral anti-immigrant groups, to attack immigrants as the ultimate hazard to blacks. As the national debate raged over illegal immigration in 2006, some blacks revived the age-old scare that illegal immigrants posed a great peril to blacks again. The issue that inflamed blacks the most, as it did decades ago, was jobs.

CHAPTER 9

Illegal Immigrants Versus Black Workers

The young black man hesitated as he stood outside the small furniture manufacturing shop in south Los Angeles in the summer of 2005. He was dressed neatly, and he was well groomed. He eyed the building warily. The sign on the narrow glass door, in English and Spanish, read "help wanted" and *trabajo aqui*. The opening was for a shop helper, mostly to sweep up and do routine cleanup and maintenance. It did not require any education or special skill. It paid minimum wage, as did many of the shops that dotted the area. The company had no employee health care plan or other benefits.

After a moment he went in and politely asked for an application. The petite receptionist, a young Latina, handed him an application form with an airy nonchalance. She curtly suggested that he fill it out and bring it back. When he asked if there would be an interview, she haltingly said only if there was a position open. The young man looked perplexed, glanced at the help wanted sign, politely thanked her and left. A couple of hours later two other young Latinos came in to apply. One was immediately hired. The other was told that another helper job might open up within the next few days. However, the workers in the shop, as they were in nearly all the other shops in the area were Latinos, a large percentage of whom were illegal immigrants.

There were no other blacks, whites or even English-speaking native-born Latino workers in the plant or in few other shops in the area. This is not a fictional story. I personally witnessed the scene at the company involving the black job seeker. Anti-illegal immigration activists say that the experience of the young black job seeker has played out thousands of times at restaurants, hotels, on farms and at manufacturing plants nationally, and that this is a major reason so many young black males are unemployed, join gangs, deal drugs and pack America's jails.

The job loss to blacks that they attribute to illegal immigration is as much perception as slight reality. However, when the perception becomes a widely-held public belief and is continually repeated as fact, it soon takes hold in public opinion. In a Pew survey taken in April 2006, just weeks after the massive immigration rights marches, more blacks than whites said that they or a family member lost or didn't get a job because the employer hired an immigrant worker. This was pure perception, since no controlled study or survey had been done as of 2006 that quantified how many blacks had actually lost jobs to immigrants. But a perception as often happens becomes reality that something has happened that adversely affects the lives of large numbers of persons, whether true or not, if enough persons believe it.

The sensitivity of blacks over jobs and illegal immigration has made even top black civil rights leaders tiptoe lightly around on the issue. Jesse Jackson has repeatedly spoken out in favor of the broadest immigration reform measures. He spoke at the giant immigrant rights march in April 2006 and unhesitatingly compared the immigrant rights movement to the civil rights movement. Yet even Jackson acknowledged that job loss was a crisis problem: "Our middle-class automotive jobs, our shipyard jobs, our steel and textile jobs were exported." Jackson quickly added, though, that those jobs didn't go to undocumented workers.

• • • • •

In 2006 Congress failed to hammer out a comprehensive immigration reform law. Even if it had succeeded, it wouldn't have conclusively answered this question: Do the estimated 10 to 12 million illegal immigrants in the country, the overwhelming majority of them Latino, take jobs from the young, the unskilled, and more often than not African-American workers at the floor level of the economy?

What if the young black job-seeker, or any other American looking for work in a low-end manufacturing plant or a restaurant in Los Angeles, was offered that a minimum wage job with few benefits and little job security? Would he or she take it? The reams of studies on the impact of illegal immigration upon American jobs give conflicting, confusing and flat-out contradictory answers. They are eagerly seized on by anti-and pro-illegal immigration reform advocates to make a case for their side.

A National Academy of Sciences study in 2002 declared that the evidence does not show that low-income workers, especially African-Americans, suffer disproportionately from the inflow of illegal immigrants. The Federation for American Immigration Reform has been the most bellicose and dogged organization in churning out reports, surveys and testimonials on the purported catastrophic damage of illegal immigration. The aim is to prove that illegal immigrants hurt low-income workers, and that African-Americans have been excised from jobs in several industries.

Economists haven't done any better in shedding insight on this contentious question. They agree that cheap illegal immigrant labor depresses wages for lower-income American workers. Harvard University economist George Borjas presents a classic case of how immigration opponents and proponents can twist and turn an economist's study on the impact of illegal immigration on American workers' jobs and wages to make their case that illegal immigration either hurts blacks or has only a marginal affect on them. "Low-skill... illegal immigration has the biggest negative impact on the wage of low-skill workers," said Borjas. "A disproportionate number of these low-skill workers happen to be minorities." He lists Hispanics and other immigrants, along with blacks, as those whom illegal immigration hurts.

Borjas' study was subject to much interpretation by the dueling immigration factions. He never says that illegal immigration directly slashed the jobs that blacks might want; only that it depresses wages in some industries. Nonetheless, he's been quoted more than any other economist by both sides on this issue to make their points that immigration either helps or hurts unskilled American workers.

Economists have frequently reversed gear on this issue. They say that if cheap immigrant labor weren't available, many industries would shut down and there wouldn't be any jobs for anybody. University of California economist David

Card singled out textiles and some farm industries, and said that they would fold completely without immigrant labor.

It's certainly hard to imagine a young black from south Los Angeles, Harlem, Boston's Roxbury district or the south side of Chicago, not to mention a native-born young white from the upscale New York City suburb of Scarsdale, or from a blue-collar neighborhood in Akron, Ohio going out to the fields to pick strawberries for 10 to 12 hours a day in the hot sun at minimum or even sub-minimum wages. Or that they'd take a job at a car wash or bus dishes in a restaurant. But what if the farm contractors, car wash owners and manufacturers paid a living wage and provided benefits? It might be a different story, at least for some marginal-skilled or unemployed young people in some poor black neighborhoods.

But when employers give the quick brush-off to young blacks and other young American workers who are willing to take lower-end jobs, they send the not-so-subtle message that they are not wanted or welcome. This is a powerful disincentive for them to pursue work in these areas of the job market. The end result is that an entire category of jobs on the ground rung of American industry is clearly marked as "Latino only."

Then there's the regional factor. There is some evidence that young workers, especially teens, will work low-wage jobs in the South and the Midwest. In Detroit, Atlanta, Baltimore and Washington, D.C., it was still not unusual to see young blacks working in hotels and restaurants in 2006. Overall, blacks still made up about forty percent of workers in food preparation, transportation and manufacturing. Even in California, where blacks have had the greatest job losses in some industries to foreign-born workers, in the 1980s, they still made up a majority or near-majority of workers in hotels and in the janitorial services.

• • • • •

The debate over whether illegal immigrants hurt young poor, unskilled American workers is not confined to low-end jobs. In 1995 Tirso del Junco, the only Latino on the U.S. Postal Services Board of Governors, ignited a modest controversy when he charged that blacks were over-represented in the post office. He cited a Government Accountability Office report on the numbers of blacks in the Los Angeles post office and aggressively called for more Latinos to be hired to correct the imbalance.

Meanwhile, starting in the late 1980s Latino employee associations in Los Angeles continued their complaints that blacks were over-represented in Los Angeles County jobs. The implication again was that more blacks in these jobs meant fewer Latinos in these jobs. The numbers bore out the complaint. There were proportionally far more blacks in county jobs than in the private sector jobs. There was a good reason for that. Blacks had waged a fierce battle during the 1960s and 1970s against discrimination in public sector hiring. A disproportionate number of blacks were employed in the public sector precisely because so many private employers still discriminated against them in their hiring. It was a question of discrimination. Yet blacks got the blame for protecting their hard-won turf in county government jobs. They had cause to resent it.

Criticism by del Junco and by Latino employee organizations of the federal government and Los Angeles county government's relative scarcity of Latinos in jobs in comparison to blacks was tantamount to a call for government agencies to skew more of their hiring toward Latinos. That touched a raw nerve with many blacks. It came on the heels of a General Accountability Office study in the early 1990s that found fewer and fewer blacks were getting jobs as janitors in Los Angeles. This was an area of work that blacks had occupied in years past. Foreign-born workers, many of them illegal immigrants, were now taking the jobs. This reinforced black fears that they were losing even more economic ground, this time not to whites but to illegal immigrants. The fears weren't totally unfounded, not that the jobs were being lost to illegal immigrants, but that the jobs were disappearing, period.

As Jackson accurately pointed out, jobs in the public sector, manufacturing and transportation have either declined or stagnated since 1995. The losses have been mostly due to federal and state budget slashes, outsourcing, and corporate and public industry downsizing. The job shrinkage has had a crippling effect on black household income. Though it has risen steadily since 1967, in 2003 it was still much less than white income, and several thousand dollars less than the median income for Hispanics. In its State of Black America report in 2006, the Urban League, found that economic conditions for the black poor and many workers had reached crisis levels.

That alarmed many blacks. "Even for blacks who are following the model of the American middle class, going to college, getting a white-collar job, " observed William Spriggs, former executive director of the National Urban League's Institute for Opportunity and Equality, "blacks have taken it on the chin. " The economic sock to the chin that many black workers took didn't go unnoticed by some Latino leaders. "We are fighting hearsay and opinion. Blacks say, 'Hey, a Latino immigrant came and took my job,' Randy Jurado Ertll, director of *El Centro de Accion Social, Inc.,* got it partly right. Some blacks did wrongly blame Latinos for losing jobs, but their net job loss during the past decade was real nonetheless.

• • • • •

The fight over jobs and illegal immigration, beginning in the mid-1990s, came at the worst possible time for the urban poor. Despite the booming economy, shrinking federal and state budgets for job training and creation programs, industry downsizing and escalating crime and violence in inner-city neighborhoods made banks and corporations even more reluctant to invest in these communities, and that made the job situation even worse. The various explanations researchers and economists gave for the drop in black income and the job losses didn't satisfy some blacks. They still blamed it on illegal immigration, and the preference of many employers to hire Latinos over blacks.

That triggered a flurry of lawsuits and complaints to the Equal Employment Opportunity Commission from some black workers. In 2002 black workers got settlements from Farmer John and Zenith International Insurance Company for allegedly being passed over for jobs that went to Latinos. The handful of suits and settlements further fed the perception that blacks were being bumped from jobs or weren't being hired in the first place because of Latinos.

Black author Claude Anderson angrily observed, "This country continues in its immigration policy to bring in an unending influx of immigrants. They're pushing blacks further and further down, making them an underclass." However, thousands of poor blacks had been pushed to and beyond the outer limit of the American economy long before illegal immigration became a hot topic and got the blame for some of the economic ills of the black poor. Anderson, as the polls amply showed, spoke for large numbers of blacks who believed that immigration was the cause of black problems and that a crackdown on it was the cure. Anderson did more than talk about the alleged damage that illegal immigration did to blacks; he joined with a handful of other blacks to help launch Choose Black America, the first black anti-immigrant lobbying group, of which more will be said later.

• • • • •

The real cure for high unemployment, of course, was more jobs. The Congressional Black Caucus and the Congressional Hispanic Caucus understood that need. They continued to push for a drastic boost in government spending on job, education and skills training programs, and to combat employment discrimination on the part of many private employers. "Problems with the immigration system cannot be resolved without looking at the larger economic needs of the nation, so that all Americans can have enhanced opportunities."

Former NAACP President Bruce Gordon's assessment of the clash between those who claimed immigrants took jobs from blacks and immigration rights advocates who claimed they didn't, was stiff and stilted, but it was accurate.

The issue is not who is taking jobs from whom, but insuring that there are enough jobs for all who want them. And even when jobs are available, the towering challenge is to prevent employers from hiding behind a mountain of racial dodges to avoid hiring young blacks, especially young black males. The challenge of combating employer discrimination was a formidable challenge long before immigration reform opponents fingered immigration as the cause for black job loss, and it still is.

CHAPTER 10

Discrimination Fuels the Job Crisis of Young Black Males

Texas Democratic Congresswoman Sheila Jackson-Lee's district in Houston has a large and growing number of Latino immigrants. This has made her one of the most outspoken advocates of liberal immigration reform. She introduced an immigration reform bill in the late 1990s that some of her fellow Congressional Black Caucus members balked at backing. Jackson-Lee sharply disputes the notion that immigrants are the reason for the tumble in black jobs. Yet in a revealing moment she expressed worry about the affect of illegal immigration on jobs: "With our communities having the highest unemployment rate, yes I can sympathize and empathize with the African-American community about what they perceive to be a population group that takes jobs."

The ambivalence and fear about jobs crashed through in a Pew Research Center poll taken during the height of the immigration reform battle in 2006. The poll found that blacks by a bigger percentage than whites were sympathetic toward the plight of illegal immigrants. The Pew poll finding backs up what other polls found: that black attitudes were far more benign toward illegal immigration than white attitudes. The Pew poll, unlike the other polls, also found that blacks, by a far bigger percentage than whites, were terrified that illegal immigrants took jobs from them.

When a group of black and Latino activists at a press conference in Los Angeles in March 2006 announced plans to hold a black and Latino unity conference that June, the press peppered them with questions about what they were going to do to allay the fears, even anger, of many blacks over immigration and jobs. The question was a good one, and for a horrible reason. The crisis of joblessness among young black males under age 30 is real, troubling and chronic. It is a major cause of the escalation in prison numbers, gang-and drug-related violence, and family instability. Illegal immigration didn't create the unemployment crisis for young black males.

The prime causes are ailing predominantly-minority public schools, massive cuts in state and federal skills-and job-training programs, persistent employer racial discrimination, and the escalating incarceration of young black men. This is particularly sensitive because the number of young blacks jailed is so high, and those numbers continue to climb. The Sentencing Project, a Washington, D.C. criminal justice system reform group, has consistently warned that America locks up more persons than any other country on the globe. In 2006, the total jailed far exceeded 2 million.

Blacks make up more than half of those imprisoned. While the chance of a white male being locked up is 1 in 25, for black males the odds soar to 1 in 3. The prospect of a young black finding a decent paying job or for that matter any job, once released is grim.

In March 2007 the Senate Joint Economic Committee squarely confronted the crisis of black male joblessness and made the tight link between high unemployment, poor education and the soaring incarceration rates for young black males. The committee made the staggering revelation that a black male without a high school diploma has a thirty percent greater chance of being imprisoned, a figure that jumps to sixty percent if he's a high school dropout. The dismal conclusion was that black males in their 20s were more likely to be in jail than in school.

Many employers didn't help matters. They refused to hire them if they had a criminal record. And many didn't even try to mask their refusal to hire ex-inmates, especially if they're black.

In a survey in 2005, New York City employers flatly told interviewers that they were less likely to hire a job applicant with a criminal record, and far less likely to hire a black applicant with a record. "Employer discrimination against minorities and ex-offenders," a survey researcher observed, "has significantly undermined job opportunities for young black men with little schooling." While having a criminal record is a major barrier to employment for marginal-educated and skilled-young blacks, employers have found even more infuriating ways to discriminate against black job seekers. They look at their names.

In 2002 researchers from MIT and the University of Chicago found that job applicants with white-sounding names were much more likely to be called for interviews than those with black-sounding names. In many cases, the black applicants had the same experience, education and skills as the white applicants. That made no difference.

In countless other studies and surveys, conducted during the past three decades, sociologists and researchers discovered that employers have concocted endless schemes to evade anti-discrimination laws. In a seven-month comprehensive university study of the hiring practices of hundreds of Chicago-area employers in the mid-1990s, many top company officials when interviewed openly said they were extremely reluctant to hire blacks.

When asked to assess the work ethic of white, black and Latino employees by race, nearly forty percent of the employers ranked blacks dead last. The employers routinely described blacks as "unskilled," "uneducated," "illiterate," "dishonest," "lacked initiative," "unmotivated," "involved with gangs and drugs," "did not understand work," "unstable," "lacked charm," "had no family values," and were "poor role models." The consensus among these employers was that blacks brought their alleged pathologies to the workplace and were to be avoided at all costs. Given the paltry wages and lack of benefits of many of these low-end jobs, many young blacks would not take these jobs even if employers did not discriminate and made these jobs available to them.

The daunting obstacles that young blacks face in the job market have little to do with illegal immigration and competition with Latino job seekers. Still, if there's any group that illegal immigration may have a damaging economic impact on, it is young black males. They still are more likely to work in and compete for jobs in industries that require marginal or no skills, such as car washes and fast food outlets. At one time, these types of jobs gave young blacks their first taste of what it was like to be in the workplace and earn some pocket money for high school and college expenses. The first job this writer got was at a car wash. I was a high school senior then. The workers at that same car wash today are exclusively Latino. Car washes and fast food joints are high on the list of the retail and service industries that employ the greatest number of illegal immigrants.

The issue and the anger over hiring illegal immigrants in low wage jobs burst open immediately after the Hurricane Katrina debacle struck New Orleans in September 2005. Even if New Orleans Mayor Ray Nagin made his foot-in-the-mouth crack that a "flood of Mexicans" could gobble up all the cleanup and reconstruction jobs in the city, black workers would still have bitterly complained that labor contractors reneged on their promise to hire them for cleanup and repair jobs in the hardest hit Gulf regions in Louisiana, Alabama and Mississippi. Instead they trucked in thousands of undocumented Latino workers. Homeland Security temporarily suspended sanctions against employers who hired undocumented workers. The Gulf Coast flap over construction jobs was no exception. According to the Pew Hispanic Research Center, illegal immigrants made up more than ten percent of the workers in the construction trades in 2005.

According to the Bureau of Labor Statistics' (BLS) population survey in the summer 2006, more than half of the nearly four million immigrant workers whom American businesses hired in the past five years have been illegal immigrants. The BLS calculated that this resulted in the loss of more than half million jobs to American-born workers, the majority of whom were under age 30. The Bureau of National Affairs, based on data from the BLS, reported that for the first time ever in 2005, the rate of unemployment for foreign-born workers fell faster than the rate of unemployment for American born workers.

The survey showed that there was a tightening tie between illegal immigration and lower wages for American workers in some industries and in some regions. It was also painful proof that illegal immigrants had displaced tens of thousands of young blacks from jobs in some low-wage industries. This posed a noticeable obstacle to young, unskilled black workers in their search for jobs. Yet, if there were no illegal immigrants to fill many of these jobs, many employers would still find countless ways to skirt discrimination laws and not hire young blacks to work them.

• • • • •

The sheer number of jobs that blacks have lost is enough for some to make an inferential case that illegal immigration has adversely affected some blacks. Immigration opponents screamed that the answer was to jail the immigrants, kick them out and militarize the border. This is inflammatory and delusional. Employers will continue to put the welcome mat out for cheap labor, illegal or otherwise, with little risk of legal sanctions. And when they can get away with it, exploit them shamelessly. Katrina was an example of that. At the same time that black workers complained that illegal immigrants took clean-up jobs from them in the Gulf area, two federal class action suits were filed that alleged that thousands of migrant workers worked brutal 12-hour shifts removing dangerous toxic wastes from buildings and were not paid.

Immigration opponents have refused to press government officials and business leaders for more job funding and training programs, and to toughen enforcement against job discrimination. That would put a dent in the job crisis among young blacks. But it would also remove the issue of black joblessness from their arsenal of weapons to bludgeon the public and elected officials on the alleged disaster of Latino illegal immigration. Immigrant rights groups are not totally blameless on this issue either. They also have not pushed openly, publicly and vigorously enough for federal and state officials and corporate officials to create more job programs and crackdown on job discrimination.

However, some unions have recognized the crucial need to build bridges between black and Latino workers who work in the lower-end, marginal or unskilled industries. The Service Employees International Union recognized the danger in pitting black and Latino workers against each other and mounted national organizing drives for union recognition and better wages and working conditions for janitors and security guards in several major cities including Los Angeles. The majority of the guards and janitors are black or Latino throughout 2006 and 2007.

This is a positive example of black and Latino workers joining forces. Union and civil rights leaders hope that their example will take root in communities that are undergoing a population transition from black to Latino and that have experienced conflicts between the two groups in recent years.

"Now is the time," insisted Salih Booker, executive director of Africa Action," to show solidarity with each other instead of being pitted against each other." The sentiment is noble and so is the effort of unions to bridge the gulf of black and brown tensions. But that doesn't diminish the crisis of black unemployment. It is very real, and business leaders and elected officials must take an honest and sober look at the possible harmful economic impact of illegal immigration on some poor, marginally skilled or unskilled blacks in some industries in some regions of the country. The undeniable fact is that there was a time when blacks were housekeepers, cooks, janitors, day laborers, and car washers filled the gritty jobs in all bottom-rung manufacturing factories and plants. Those jobs did provide young blacks such as myself their first *entree* into the labor market. It's unrealistic to think that blacks can ever fill those jobs *en masse* again. Black progress up the job ladder, a changing economy, discrimination, and yes, illegal immigration, has changed that prospect probably for good. That's far different, though, than placing the entire blame for the job crisis of young blacks on illegal immigration.

CHAPTER 11

Immigration Wars Make Strange Bedfellows

For a brief moment in late May 2006 there was a buzz of excitement among immigration reform foes in Washington, D.C. They were excited about a press conference scheduled for May 23rd by immigration reform opponents at the National Press Club. There was a twist. The press conference wouldn't feature the customary immigration reform foes—conservative Republican politicians, right-leaning think tank directors and rabid border control advocates.

The press conference was billed as the first major national effort to bring together black opponents of immigration reform. The odd assemblage included writers, preachers, a homeless rights advocate, professional anti-immigration advocates and a few local black community residents from the Washington, D.C. area, who claimed to speak for the majority of black Americans on immigration. Their name, Choose Black America (CBA), implied that blacks had already made up their minds that illegal immigration was the prime threat to them.

Speaker after speaker thundered that immigration was killing black America. They tossed out the familiar arguments that illegal immigrants had created near depression levels of unemployment among young blacks, drained scarce resources from the schools and public services, and dragged down the quality of life in poor black communities. They protested that government law enforcement agencies were giving illegal immigrants a virtual free pass to enter the country, and that employers were scared stiff to check to see if their hires were here legally. In a later mission statement, CBA indignantly blamed illegal immigrants for virtually every social ill that blacks had ever faced: "Mass illegal immigration has been the single greatest impediment to black advancement in this country over the past 25 years." It was a big, brash, sweeping and volatile charge. It was clearly designed to stir passions, but it was no different from what avowed immigration reform opponents had been saying repeatedly in every public venue for years.

Choose Black America members pledged to pull out all stops to derail the immigration reform bill in Congress. Frank Morris, Sr., the group's chair, told reporters afterward, "We are here to sound the alarm." Another participant beamed to reporters that blacks were calling them from all over the country and wanted to know how they could join the group.

This was not a spontaneous gathering of public-spirited blacks outraged over the effect of illegal immigration. The Federation for American Immigration Reform (FAIR) paid for the airfare, hotel accommodations and expenses for most of the participants as well as the rental fee for the press conference facility. The organization has long demanded the toughest possible immigration laws and the tightest possible border control enforcement. Morris was a board member of FAIR. The CBA was only the latest in a string of front groups that FAIR bankrolled to push its agenda. Others included You Don't Speak for Me, and American Latino Voices Speaking Out Against Illegal Immigration.

Though CBA grabbed a few lines in the national press and churned out a few press releases, as a visible presence on the anti-immigration movement scene it was virtually dead on arrival. The participants had made their point that there some noted blacks were willing to put their bodies and faces in front of a camera to oppose immigration reform. They were not afraid of being branded bigots in the process. FAIR seemed to have gotten its money's worth from the conference and the participants.

Meanwhile, a week later, and two thousand miles away, a spirited community forum was held in south Los Angeles on black and Latino relations. Near the close of the session, a young black man in the audience stood up and proudly, even defiantly, shouted that he was a member of the Minuteman Project. Instead of being shouted down, many blacks in the audience shook their heads in agreement.

• • • • •

At first glance it seemed absolutely ridiculous that Minuteman Project leaders would pick a park in a predominantly black neighborhood in Los Angeles as a jump-off point for their national caravan to Washington, D.C. in May 2006. The caravan planned to stop in 13 cities including President Bush's hideout in Crawford, Texas. Since 2005 when the Minutemen first toted their cameras, beach chairs and binoculars to the Arizona-Mexico border to shame politicians into taking action to stop illegal immigration, they have been roundly criticized as a racist organization.

Minuteman Project leaders cringed at the charge. They claimed they did everything to shoo racists away from their organization, and that the FBI did background checks on potential members (The FBI denied the claim). They also claimed to have a multi-ethnic diverse membership.

Yet the avowed white supremacist National Alliance group, Neo-Nazis, and an assortment of kooks, cranks and crazies flocked to the border in 2005 to join Minuteman protests. On the white power website, *Stormfront* a National Alliance activist implored the "white nationalist community" to back the Minuteman Project.

The Minutemen had almost no black support before the massive immigration marches in March 2006, and their presence was nil in black communities. They were denounced by mainstream civil rights organizations and black elected officials because they had taken no public stand on issues such as affordable health care, failing public schools, police misconduct, the extension of the 1965 Voting Rights Act and the astronomically high black male unemployment rate. These are issues that are of greatest concern to blacks. The Minuteman website was filled with xenophobic, nativist, borderline, race-tinged code word taunts at the "invasion" of "hordes" of "illegal aliens." This ignited a brief flurry of anti-immigrant, and worse, anti-Latino bashing, as well as reports of taunts, harassment and physical assaults on some Latinos in Texas, California and Florida.

Minuteman leaders sensed a window of opportunity in the growing number of blacks who expressed unease and rage over the huge numbers of Latinos who marched in the streets and demanded amnesty and virtually open borders.

The Minutemen's pitch to blacks was a shrewd, cynical ploy to capitalize on the split among blacks over illegal immigration in order to link immigration with black joblessness and poverty. Minuteman leaders tapped into the anger and anxiety of some blacks over the economic plummet of poor blacks by pandering to their tough-on-crime sentiment, and eventually managed to rally a handful of black supporters to their cause. The Minuteman Project set an ambitious goal of 500 new chapters nationally by 2006 and over one million new members. They came nowhere near getting those numbers. However, the Anti-Defamation League, in an alarmed report on hate groups in America in January 2007, found that the anti-immigration backlash stirred a resurgence in the ugly fortunes of the Klan and other far right wing extremist groups.

The Minutemen, though always careful to disavow the racists among them, remained passionately convinced that the majority of Americans agreed with them that illegal immigration was a plague on American society and that only harsh employer sanctions, tough criminal penalties and the militarizing of the border were the only ways to eliminate it.

They banked that thousands of blacks agreed with them

and that they would ride with them in their flag-festooned autos and caravan to Washington in protest. That didn't happen, at least not in the big numbers that the Minuteman Project had hoped for. The few blacks who rode in cars with a group that had said nothing and done nothing to promote civil rights or fight poverty, as well as their checkered ties with dubious groups, proved that immigration had conjured up strange alliances.

• • • • •

The attraction of the Minuteman Project to some disgruntled blacks was more than just a visceral and emotional reaction to the congressional battle over immigration reform. The signs that illegal immigration had touched a sore nerve in many blacks were there all along. In fact, the first big warning sign of black frustration with illegal immigration came during the battle over Proposition 187 in California in 1994. White voters voted by big margins for the proposition that denied public services to undocumented immigrants. Nearly fifty percent of blacks also backed the measure.

Republican governor Pete Wilson shamelessly pandered to anti-immigrant hysteria and rode it to a re-election victory. Wilson also got nearly 20 percent of the black vote in the 1994 election. It was double what Republicans in California typically had gotten from blacks. Wilson bumped up his black vote total with his freewheeling assault on illegal immigration. Blacks have also given substantial support to anti-bilingual ballot measures in California.

More than a decade later black attitudes toward illegal immigrants, who almost always are seen as Latino illegal immigrants, were put to the electoral test in Arizona with another ballot initiative. Proposition 200 mandated tough sanctions on employers for hiring illegal immigrants and tighter border enforcement. Exit polls showed that more than 65 percent of blacks backed the measure. It passed by a landslide just as Proposition 187 in California had done a decade before.

• • • • •

As the battle-lines firmed on immigration reform, some black conservatives quickly jumped into the fray. A few months before the 2004 presidential election, Project 21, the Washington, D.C.-based group of black conservative businesspersons and professionals, chastised Bush for his conflicted immigration reform proposals. The group protested that if Congress enacted Bush's proposals it would flood the country with swarms of illegal immigrants, speed the deterioration in public education, further bulge the prisons, and undercut American workers' wages.

That continued to be the standard charge made black and white immigration reform opponents.

In the following two years, Project 21 was mute on the immigration issue, but the renewed immigration reform battle in Congress stirred them to action. They were especially outraged that immigration reform advocates equated immigrant rights with the civil rights movement. In a press statement the group declared, "The civil rights movement was about some American citizens being treated worse than others. The immigration rallies are about lawbreaking non-citizens wanting the same rights and benefits as legal citizens."

Project 21's greatest horror, however, as with all the other black immigration reform foes, was that illegal immigrants depressed wages, elbowed blacks out of low-skilled and unskilled farm and manufacturing jobs and snatched vital services from the black poor.

Project 21, the black Minutemen, and Choose Black America organizers demanded that Congress crack down on illegal immigrants, and they implored blacks to pound away on Congress to back up their demand. That was mostly for public consumption. The chances of blacks in any large numbers aggressively lobbying Congress to oppose immigration reform proposals were nil. Neither Project 21 nor the black Minutemen had the resources, organization, cohesion, or political will to mobilize blacks in large numbers to fight illegal immigration. They had no real means to counter mainstream civil rights organizations and the Congressional Black Caucus, which had by now backed to the hilt liberal immigration reform.

Civil rights leaders and the Congressional Black Caucus went even further. They now repeatedly condemned the thinly disguised race-tinged appeals of the Minuteman Project, Save Our State, and the legions of other edgy anti-immigration groups that had cropped up in nearly every part of the country. Despite the political muscle of the civil rights groups and black Democrats, and the puny efforts of the handful of vocal black immigration reform opponents to rally blacks to fight immigration reform, they faced a dilemma.

The immigration debate continued to be the subject of intense debate both within and without Congress and in the states. With so many young blacks unemployed and with a prison cell staring many of them in the face, more immigrant-bashing front groups such as Choose Black America could pop up. More than a few blacks then might find it harder to resist the temptation to join them, or at least continue to harangue illegal immigrants.

In a final, maybe even fitting touch of madcap irony to the Minuteman Project's open appeals to blacks, Minuteman Project co-founder Jim Gilchrist, who organized the raucous anti-immigration rally at a park in a black neighborhood in Los Angeles in May 2006, was ousted from the group in December 2006 after a bitter dispute over alleged financial bungling and media grandstanding. The organization hand-picked Marvin Stewart, a minister and an African-American, to take over the presidency from Gilchrist. "I have to take a moral high ground," Stewart self-righteously intoned. That didn't change this fact: The color of the face at the top of the organization may have changed with Stewart's takeover of the leadership, but the membership didn't. It was still mostly white and conservative. It is yet another warning sign that the immigration wars indeed make strange bedfellows.

The willingness of some blacks to join the Minuteman Project, and to even embrace their philosophy, paled in comparison to the even greater internal debate among blacks over whether the immigration reform movement could be compared to the civil rights movement. It seemed nearly every black had an opinion about that, and their opinion told as much about how blacks viewed the civil rights movement as it did how they viewed the immigration reform movement.

CHAPTER 12

Packaging Immigration as The New Civil Rights Movement

"African-Americans during the civil rights movement were in search of the American dream and that's what our movement is trying to achieve for our community. We face the same issues even if we speak different languages." Jaime Contreras, a first-generation immigrant from El Salvador and the president of the National Capital Immigration Coalition, spoke a few days after tens of thousands of immigrant rights demonstrators took to the streets in New York demanding that Congress break its stalemate and pass the more moderate immigration reform bill. Contreras had something else in mind when he compared the immigrant rights battle with the old black-led 1960s civil rights movement. It was a not-so-subtle rebuke of those blacks who were enraged at any comparison of the two movements. He got it almost right.

The 1960s civil rights movement was a frantic search by blacks to force America to live up to its promise of justice and equality. That's the dream of many in the immigration rights movement as well. This is what has pricked a sore nerve among many blacks. This was plainly evident during the massive march of tens of thousands in Los Angeles and other cities for immigrant rights in March 2006. The old mainstream civil rights groups, at least initially, were virtually mute on immigration and the marches. There were no position papers, statements or press releases on the websites of the NAACP, the Urban League or the Southern Christian Leadership Conference on immigration reform or the marches. The Congressional Black Caucus didn't do much better. It issued a perfunctory, tepid and cautious statement opposing the draconian provisions of the House bill that passed in December 2005.

The bill called for a wall on the southern border, a massive beef-up in border security and tough sanctions on employers who hired illegal aliens. The Senate later wrestled

with the bill but eventually threw in the towel and failed to
pass it when many senators raised deep reservations about
some of the harsh enforcement provisions. The Senate tried
again briefly revived the bill in May 2007. But it was still no
go on passage.

Only nine Congressional Black Caucus (CBC) members
initially backed the relatively liberal immigration reform bill
introduced by CBC member Sheila Lee Jackson in 2004. They
were politicians and they read the political tea leaves—in this
case, the polls in which many blacks expressed grave doubts
about illegal immigration—and the politicians moved cau-
tiously on the issue. The early silence and caution of mainstream civil rights groups and the CBC's modest support for
immigrant rights was a radical departure from the past.

During the 1980s, when immigration was not the top
issue of national public policy debate that it became in 2006,
the Caucus in 1985 staunchly opposed tougher immigration
proposals, voted against employer sanctions for hiring illegal
immigrants, and an English language requirement to attain
legalization. That was an easy call then. Those were the White
House years of President Ronald Reagan. He signed the reform bill in 1986. Since then, conservative Republicans took
the cue from him and have pushed over the years for even
more restrictive immigration laws. Civil rights leaders and
black Democrats then waged a low-yield war against Rea-

gan's policies. A stronger immigration reform law was one of them.

The NAACP made a slight nod to the immigration fight when it invited Hector Flores, President of the League of United Latin American Citizens, to address its 2002 convention. The NAACP billed the invitation as an "historic first." In his talk, Flores clearly recognized the importance of the overture and the prospect of the two groups working together: "No one organization or group can go it alone and where our interests meet, we stand ready to work with the NAACP and others in an equitable fashion."

The NAACP, though, was careful to note that immigration was one of a list of policy initiatives the two groups would work together on. That list included support for affirmative action, expanded hate crimes legislation, voting rights protections and increased health and education funding. Just how or by what means the NAACP and Flores' group would work together on these problems was left dangling for the time being.

• • • • •

There were two reasons the Congressional Black Caucus and civil rights leaders initially treaded lightly on the immigrant rights battle. They were loath to equate the immigrant rights movement with the civil rights battles of the 1960s. They saw immigrant rights as a reactive,

narrow, single-issue movement whose leaders had not actively reached out to black leaders and groups. Spanish language
newspapers and radio stations, such as *La Opinion, Hoy, Tu
Azteca, Telemundo, Univision* and the popular DJs drove the
mammoth march and rally in Los Angeles in March 2006.
They implored protestors *"a las calles"* and other chants in
Spanish. Though they did not openly urge protestors to wave
Mexican and El Salvadoran flags and the flags of their former
countries, the marchers waved them and they were not initially discouraged to do so.

The graphic display of nationalist sentiment irked many
blacks, and that caused some black leaders to note the chorus
of anger that continued to rise from many African-Americans, especially the black poor, of whom a significant number outright opposed amnesty and full civil rights for illegal
immigrants. The fear, anger and resentment among many
blacks toward the immigrant rights movement could have at
least in part been dampened if immigrant rights groups had
done a better job of reaching out to civil rights groups. That
meant reassuring them that they would fight for jobs and justice for poor blacks, too. Other than a speech or two by Jesse
Jackson and other civil rights leaders at the marches and a
few veteran civil rights activists who marched in the protests,
there was little attempt to involve blacks in the planning, let
alone incorporate their worry about black job losses in the
marchers' demands.

The Congressional Hispanic Caucus, Mexican American Legal Defense and Education Fund, the National Council of La Raza, and the League of United Latin American Citizens issued press statements, position papers and statements in support of civil rights issues. But they are politicians and civil rights groups, and that is their duty. That is not the case with immigrant rights groups. Their leaders were conspicuously missing at rallies and gatherings on issues that blacks find important, including renewal of certain parts of the 1965 Voting Rights Act that were due to expire in 2007, police misconduct, improving failing inner city public schools, and most importantly, the profound crisis of black male joblessness.

The NAACP's mission statement reads: "The mission of the National Association for the Advancement of Colored People is to ensure the political, educational, social and economic equality of rights of all persons and to eliminate racial hatred and racial discrimination." The statement is in sharp contrast to the mission statement of the Mexican American Political Association. Its mission statement reads: "The Mexican American Political Association (MAPA), founded in Fresno, California in 1960, has been, and is, dedicated to the constitutional and democratic principle of political freedom and representation for the Mexican and Hispanic people of the United States of America." MAPA has been a major backer of the immigrant rights protests, but has not spoken out continually and vigorously on black rights issues. And in its mission statement there is no mention of blacks, poor whites or even other non-Latino immigrant groups, just Latinos.

That omission and disconnect between the civil rights organizations and immigrant rights groups could have been avoided, and there was a way. Three years earlier in 2003 civil rights activists and immigrant rights leaders barnstormed to nine American cities, drumming up support for immigrant rights. They used the model of the old freedom rides that black protestors used in the 1960s to attack legal segregation. Immigrant rights groups could have used the same model in 2006 but didn't, and because they didn't, it appeared to black leaders that immigration rights organizations were narrow, exclusionary and even hostile to blacks.

That increased confusion and fueled the anger of some leading black politicians. California Assemblyman Mervyn Dymally came out in support of humane immigration reform. Dymally, born in Trinidad, and the first foreign-born black member of Congress, in a statement on his Web site in May 2006 said, "While I have not participated in any of the demonstrations because I was never invited by the organizers to do so, Assembly member Joe Coto, vice-chair of the California Legislative Latino Caucus, knows of my support for the demonstrations."

The lack of an interracial message in the fight for civil rights was disturbing, and it opened the door even wider for black immigration foes to assail immigration reform and denounce the civil rights leaders who supported it. When black members of the Minuteman Project held their protest in a predominantly black neighborhood in Los Angeles in May 2006, immigrant activist and MAPA president Nativo Lopez said that he believed they were out of step with most black leaders and that both blacks and Hispanics face the same problems. He was partly correct. Mainstream civil rights organizations condemned the Minuteman Project as narrow, bigoted and opportunistic. And only a handful of blacks have been active in the group. But Lopez did not acknowledge the undercurrent of unease and hostility of many blacks to immigrant rights, and even more worrisome, toward Latinos. That would have been too painful and too politically incorrect to recognize.

• • • • •

Historians, politicians and civil rights activists have hailed the March on Washington in August 1963 as the watershed event in the civil rights movement. It defined an era of protest, sounded the death knell for nearly a century of legal segregation and challenged Americans to make racial justice a reality for blacks.

Yet the estimated million who marched and held rallies for immigrant rights in Los Angeles in 2006 and other cities dwarfed the estimated quarter million persons at the March on Washington. If the numbers and passion that immigration reform stirs mean anything, the judgment of history will be that it also defined an era, sounded the ending bell for discrimination against immigrants, and challenged Americans to make justice and equality a reality for immigrants, both legal and illegal.

Even so, the immigrant rights movement had another side to it, one that was less racially correct. This side sparked controversy. It ignited potent emotions among blacks and publicly exposed the split between mainstream civil rights leaders and the Congressional Black Caucus on immigration reform. It also exposed the tensions that at times plague black and Latino relations. Many blacks declared the movement a threat to their interests and rejected the position of the civil rights leaders who backed immigration reform.

Despite its initial silence and reservations about immigration reform, the NAACP issued a set of principles that affirmed its opposition to the House's punitive immigration bill, called for the most liberal reform possible of the immigration laws and deemed the immigration rights movement a civil rights struggle. This only infuriated the black immigration reform opponents further. They continued to harangue the NAACP, Jesse Jackson and other civil rights leaders as traitors and sellouts.

The one thing that they continued to especially bristle at

was the comparison to the civil rights movement. "The civil rights movement was a fight for justice and equality," Deneen Moore angrily said. "Illegal immigrants are fighting the rule of the law." Moore was a member of Project 21, and she echoed their sentiment and that of thousands of other blacks who wanted the most restrictive immigration law possible.

Nevertheless, the battle over immigrant rights will continue to be fought as fiercely and doggedly in the coming years as the civil rights battles of the 1960s. Those battles forever altered the way Americans look at race. The immigrant rights battle will profoundly alter the way Americans look at immigrants. Civil rights leaders eventually got over their initial hesitancy to see that, but to their credit, when they did, they tossed their full support to the reform fight. It was, after all, as were the civil rights struggles of the 1960s, a struggle for justice and fairness.

Another issue loomed large in 2004. It was more than an issue of justice and fairness. It was an issue of life and death. The Iraq war posed another challenge to blacks and Latinos. Blacks, and especially Latinos, made up a significant percent of the fighting forces in Iraq. Latinos also made up a disproportionate percentage of the battlefield casualties. Latinos and blacks in the early days of the war saw the war quite differently. The majority of blacks vehemently opposed it while the majority of Latinos backed it. That exposed for a brief time a crucial life and death public policy issue. The war in Iraq.

CHAPTER 13

Iraq War Divided Blacks and Latinos Too

A malia Avila did not support the Iraq war. Yet she didn't hesitate in describing her joyous feelings the day that her son Victor Gonzalez joined the Marines: "I was so proud of him. It was a beautiful day." Avila is a Mexican immigrant whose son was born in Salinas, California. His enlistment, for her as for many other Latino immigrants whose sons and daughters continue to sign up in record numbers with the military despite the war, is a point of pride. In U.S. Army post-enlistment surveys, Latinos list "patriotism" and "service to country" as far and away the main reasons for enlisting. That's a sharp contrast to blacks, who have increasingly disdained military service, and who from the opening gun of the Iraq war have loudly opposed it.

The first year after President Bush launched his failed and flawed war in Iraq in 2003, the pollsters got busy. Practically every month they measured American attitudes toward the war. It was no surprise that far more blacks than whites opposed the war. Many blacks believe that they fight and die in greater numbers than whites in America's wars, even though with the arguable exception of the Vietnam War, the death toll for blacks in America's wars has not been disproportionate to that of whites. The belief that it was higher has prompted blacks to oppose the Iraq war by a far bigger margin than whites.

The big surprise was the wide gulf between blacks and Latinos on the war. Civil rights leaders and Latino activists strongly protested the war. Many members of the Congressional Black Caucus and the Congressional Hispanic Caucus overwhelmingly opposed the congressional resolution in October 2003 that gave Bush authorization to attack Iraq. A Pew Research Center poll in February 2004 found that a sizeable number of Latinos, and an even bigger number of American-born Latinos, supported the war. Less than half of the blacks in the poll supported the war.

Two years later the number of blacks opposing the war

had nearly doubled. By that time more than 90 percent of blacks not only opposed the war, they said they would discourage their sons and daughters from joining the army if it meant supporting the war. This was a radical break from the past when blacks were among the most rousing advocates of military service during America's wars. They saw military service as a way to prove their loyalty and patriotism, and hoped that this would hasten the end of Jim Crow segregation.

The wide gap between blacks and Latinos was vividly underscored in Los Angeles on the first anniversary of the war when hundreds of blacks held an antiwar rally. Meanwhile, across town, Latino war veterans and community residents staged a pro-war rally at a memorial site in East Los Angeles named after Raul Morin, a Mexican-American writer, who wrote about Mexican-American Medal of Honor awardees. A close look at the reasons that many more blacks than whites also opposed the war also tells why blacks and Latinos also differ on the war, at least initially.

While the majority of Latinos are Democrats, a sizeable and growing number aren't. In Texas and Florida, nearly one-third of Latinos voted for Bush in 2000. With the departure of former Oklahoma Congressman J.C. Watts from Congress in 2004, there was not a single black GOP member of Congress. All Congressional Black Caucus members are Democrats. However, Congressional Latinos are politically divided. Most are Democrats, but some are Republicans who have branded the Congressional Hispanic Caucus as too liberal and activist.

Yet the widespread support-the-troops-if-not-the war-itself, sentiment among Latinos spurred Xavier Bacerra, the former chair of the Congressional Hispanic Caucus, a centrist Democrat and no Bush cheerleader, to join with a conservative Republican congressman in co-sponsoring a congressional resolution in 2004 urging support for the troops. In contrast, on the same day two ranking members of the Congressional Black Caucus, Sheila Jackson Lee and John Conyers, introduced a failed resolution demanding that Bush justify his war policy to Congress.

• • • • •

According to Department of Defense figures, Latinos are in even greater danger on the battlefield than blacks. They make up nearly 20 percent of army and Marine frontline combat units. In the opening days of the Iraq war, six Latinos were listed as killed or captured. Latino activists say this is another reason that Latinos should oppose the war. However, the battlefield risks have also kindled patriotism and pride among many Latinos. Even the many Latinos—-and that includes recent immigrants—-who oppose or are conflicted on the war, still regard the army as a true testing ground to prove loyalty to a country they widely regard as a bastion of freedom and liberty.

With the spectacular surge in education and wealth among blacks and with more blacks in business and the professions than ever, the military is no longer the exclusive ticket out of the ghetto for many blacks. For many young Latinos, the military is still a prime place to acquire skills and training and for career advancement. Latinos are younger than other groups and therefore they make up a sizeable number of military eligible youth. During the mid-1990s, Secretary of Army Louis Caldera, a Latino, prodded the army to intensify its recruitment efforts among Latinos. While ROTC programs were being eliminated or chased away from major universities and colleges, Junior ROTC programs flourished at many predominantly Latino high schools in Los Angeles and other cities.

• • • • •

At the Los Angeles rally to support the troops, several participants spoke with reverence and respect of Marine Cpl. Jose Gutierrez, a recent immigrant from Guatemala. Gutierrez, it was believed, was the second soldier to die in battle in Iraq. There was no honor in his death for the noted New York attorney Raul Reyes: "Every soldier killed in Iraq leaves behind a broken family, and for Hispanics *la familia* is the sacred unit of our culture," he declared. The heavy losses to Latinos demanded that they give one message to Bush, Reyes contended: "The message from the majority of Hispanics is clear." *Ya.* Enough. *No mas* Joses."

Indeed, as the deaths mounted and more Latinos filled those body bags coming back from Iraq, the majority of Latinos increasingly soured on the war. In a Pew Research Center Poll in December 2006, a huge majority of Latinos opposed the war and thought the U.S. should get out. Even then, many more Latinos were not quite ready to totally denounce the war effort. One third of Latinos polled still said good things about, if not the war, the military.

The military still kindled patriotism and pride among many Latinos. Military recruiters will continue to sell the army to young Latinos, especially recent immigrants, as the one place where "they can be all they can be." But the high Latino death rate on the battlefield, and the often-failed promise that they would get top-level training and education, badly mocked that claim. Though Latinos made up less than 10 percent of Army personnel in 2001, they still made up nearly twenty percent of the combat troops and nearly twelve percent of the combat deaths in Iraq.

In the beginning months of the fighting, the Iraq war created another racial division between blacks and whites. But it also created at least momentarily one between blacks and Latinos. The mounting death toll, the lack of a firm plan to end the war, and the painful toll the deaths took on Latino families quickly turned the majority of Latinos against the war. In fact, many now saw it as a bigger problem than the economy or even immigration.

Anti-war sentiment notwithstanding, many Latinos still clung to the belief that the military was a prime testing ground to prove loyalty and devotion to the country and the flag. Blacks had no such illusion about the military. More black leaders, such as Congressional Black Caucus chairperson Carolyn Cheeks Kilpatrick, weren't afraid to say so: "We want the war ended, and we want our troops out of there."

The divide on the war between blacks and Latinos was yet another example that racial issues can't be neatly packaged in black and white, and that included the issue of war and peace as well. Eventually, the majority of Latinos came to see that Bush's war was a no-win, wasteful and deadly exercise in futility. They joined with blacks and the majority of other Americans in opposing it. In the end, blacks and Latinos found common ground on ending a war that put many of their sons and daughters in mortal danger. That was a good thing.

Conclusion

At a planning summit in Atlanta for his Poor Peoples' March in March 1968, Dr. Martin Luther King, Jr. quizzically turned to one of his aides and asked, "Tijerina who?" The Tijerina in question was Reies Lopez Tijerina. A year earlier, Tijerina had rocketed to national fame when he and a band of armed men had taken over a courthouse in New Mexico, demanding land rights for Mexican farm workers.

Though King was puzzled at who Tijerina was, he eagerly sought an accommodation with him and other Latino leaders. He urged them to play a more forthright role in the march. King wanted Latinos, blacks, American Indians and poor whites to march in lockstep for civil rights and economic justice. King, however, was virtually a lone voice calling for such an alliance.

Many in King's inner circle of black ministers and ac-

tivists grumbled openly that black leaders must be the absolute leaders in the Poor People's March. Their meaning was
clear. Blacks had done the marching, picketing, demonstrat-
ing, fighting and dying for civil rights. Racism affected blacks
more deeply and profoundly than any other group. To them,
the struggle for land and immigrant rights by Mexicans was
a sideshow struggle that did not have the glitter, glamour or
poignancy of the black struggle. They regarded Latinos and
other ethnic groups at best as subservient partners who were
welcome as long as they knew their place. The most crass and
cynical of King's black advisors regarded Latinos as interlop-
ers who benefited from the black struggle but had contributed nothing to it.

At a planning staff meeting, a campaign advisor bluntly
said, "I do not think I am at the point where a Mexican can
sit in and call strategy on a steering committee." It was pa-
ternalistic, offensive, and condescending. The remark totally
demeaned Latinos and the importance of their struggle. Tijerina and other Latino leaders chafed at the slight, and some
refused to participate in the March. Those who came made
it clear that their struggle against racism, for land and farm
worker rights, and for cultural identity was just as important
as that of blacks. They demanded that they be recognized
and respected as leaders. The rift was temporarily smoothed
over, and Tijerina and other Latino leaders agreed to join the
March and took up residence at Resurrection City, the offi-

cial name given to the Poor People's March encampment in Washington, D.C.

• • • • •

There were other events that had a profound affect on ethnic relations in America. King's murder, the collapse of the civil rights movement, and the self-destruct of the Black Power movement brought fragmentation and disillusionment to black organizations. At the close of the 1980s King and the handful of other black activists who saw the fight of first and second generation Latinos, both native-born and recent immigrants, as a fight for civil rights and economic justice that was as important as the struggle of that of blacks, were dead or had long since retired from civil rights activism. That leadership vacuum marked the start by many blacks of the retreat to racial withdrawal.

By the 1990s the steady rise in the number of immigrants, legal and illegal, had radically changed the shape of ethnic politics in America. The number of illegal immigrants soared from an estimated three million to five million in 1990 to double-digit numbers a decade later. Many now worked jobs in cities such as Detroit, Chicago, Washington, D.C. and Atlanta that were majority black or where blacks made up a significant percentage of the population. In those cities Latinos made up the largest number of illegal immigrants that worked in the lower-skilled and wage jobs.

By 2004, Latinos displaced blacks as the largest non-white minority in America, and that alarmed more blacks. They bitterly complained that Latinos were overcrowding what had formerly been exclusively black neighborhoods and running down achievement standards in the schools. The issue that pricked the sorest spot was jobs. Blacks shouted that illegal immigrants had booted them out of unskilled entry-level jobs in hotels, restaurants and car washes. Generations of black students and black unskilled workers had used these jobs as a stepping-stone up the economic ladder to better paying, skilled jobs and the professions, or to help defray their expenses while attending college.

Immigrant rights groups countered that these were jobs that blacks wouldn't take anyway, and in bashing Latinos, blacks were unfairly scapegoating them for their loss of economic ground. By then, the memory of black and Latino co-operation that had marked the Poor Peoples' March had long since faded. For too many blacks and Latinos, that example of ethnic cooperation no longer seemed relevant anyway.

They were wrong. Despite its towering logistical problems, mishaps and ideological rifts, the March still ranks as the best effort black and Latino leaders have made to weld an alliance to fight for civil rights and economic justice. For King and the small band of black visionary activists, injustice was injustice, and it didn't matter whether the victim was an American-born black or a foreign-born Latino. For that too brief moment in history, the Poor Peoples' March meshed the old civil rights movement for black rights with a broader movement for the civil rights of other minorities.

· · · · ·

There were other signs that the ideal of black and Latino cooperation on the formidable problems of poverty and discrimination was still alive. A few days after then-Mexican President Vicente Fox ignited a firestorm in 2005 with his remark that Mexican immigrants will work jobs that blacks won't, Jesse Jackson and Ann Marie Tallman, the president and general counsel of MALDEF, met privately in Atlanta. The immediate reason for the meeting was Fox's remarks. Tallman sensed the potential damage they could do to the fragile outreach efforts the organization had made to black groups to fight jointly for affirmative action and voting rights, and against job discrimination. Jackson and Tallman had another objective in getting together. That objective went far beyond simply condemning Fox's remarks. The president had given them a much-needed opening to form a real, working coalition to work on the issues that impacted blacks and Latinos.

"We must move toward building a coalition that seeks

reconciliation not confrontation," Jackson somberly told the press. Jackson's brief summary statement on what the coalition should achieve told much about the peril and the promise of black and Latino relations. Jackson also warned that corporate interests would try to keep blacks and Latinos at odds with each other and that they should not let the corporations use them as pawns and scapegoats. Tallman struck a similar chord: "In times of controversy and conflict there are opportunities to show courage and leadership."

Tallman and Jackson promised that they'd hold roundtables with business, labor and civil rights groups at future dates in 2005 to itemize the specifics on their plan to combat racial problems. Unfortunately, the promise of an active coalition the two leaders made wasn't kept. There was no indication that the roundtables were held, or if they were held, that anything came out of them of practical value. It was another opportunity missed to build the much talked about black and Latino coalition at a national level. Even if they had succeeded in making good on their promise, it still left hanging how roundtables could or would change the perception among many blacks that immigration reform worsened their plight.

This was a stumbling block, but it didn't have to totally unhinge efforts by blacks and Latinos to work together. The several hundred black and Latino civil rights activists, union organizers, politicians and educators who met in Los

Angeles in June 2006 were determined to try to find a way around that block. They mostly avoided the minefield debate over the pros and cons of immigration reform and pledged to work together on common problems such as the lack of jobs, quality education, and affordable health care, and combating gang violence. Maria Elena Durazo, then-director of the L.A. County Federation of Labor, quickly tried to remove the stumbling block created by the rancor over immigration when she promised that the unions would step up their efforts to recruit and hire more blacks in hotels and restaurants and in other service industries.

Christine Chavez, another conference participant, had projected a vision of black and Latino unity that harked back to the vision that her grandfather Cesar Chavez and Dr. King had held, fought for and repeatedly praised each other for four decades before: "I think both of our communities realize that we're fighting over crumbs when we should be asking for a bigger piece of the pie together."

Much had happened, both good and bad, on the rocky road of black and Latino relations, since King and Chavez, the two biggest and brightest icons of the black and Latino fight for justice and economic uplift in America, had projected that vision to the nation, and Christine Chavez had just made the same call for unity. For a moment on that June day in Los Angeles in 2006, that vision of unity still burned brightly.

Diverging Views in Black and Brown of Immigration

The open and latent tensions between many blacks and Latinos exploded to the surface during the immigration battle in Congress in early 2006. The view of blacks and Latinos wildly diverged on how they saw immigration affecting race, politics, and American life. But how divergent were those views. Black America Web sought the answer from blacks and the Pew

Research Center sought the answer from Latinos. The diverging views represented perhaps the biggest challenge of all to blacks and Latinos.

BAW Immigration Poll Results.

Who would benefit most from a more pro-immigration policy?

American industries that hire cheap labor: 43 percent

Mexican-Americans, Latinos: 24 percent

Mexico: 21 percent

The United States: 18 percent

The Republican Party: 7 percent

African, Caribbean, Haitian immigrants: 4 percent

The Democratic Party: 3 percent

Black Americans: 2 percent

None of the above: 7 percent

Illegal immigrants are taking jobs away from low-income blacks.

Agree: 28 percent

Slightly agree: 28 percent

Not sure: 8 percent

Slightly disagree: 17 percent

Disagree: 19 percent

Illegal immigrants are doing jobs that blacks and other Americans won't do.

Agree: 31 percent

Slightly agree: 21 percent

Not sure: 7 percent

Slightly disagree: 13 percent

Disagree: 23 percent

The pro-immigrant agenda does not serve the black community.

Agree: 44 percent

Slightly agree: 21 percent

Not sure: 23 percent

Slightly disagree: 8 percent

Disagree: 5 percent

Tension in my community between blacks and the growing illegal immigrant community is increasing.

Agree: 15 percent

Slightly agree: 17 percent

Not sure: 28 percent

Slightly disagree: 14 percent

Disagree: 25 percent

Congress should make it easier for illegal immigrants to become U.S. citizens.

Agree: 9 percent

Slightly agree: 14 percent

Not sure: 12 percent

Slightly disagree: 19 percent

Disagree: 45 percent

People of color ultimately have the same concerns and agendas, so the black community benefits as immigrant rights expand.

Agree: 12 percent

Slightly disagree: 18 percent

Not sure: 20 percent

Slightly disagree: 18 percent

Disagree: 31 percent

The concerns raised by illegal immigration are minor compared to the benefits we gain as a nation.

Agree: 11 percent

Slightly agree: 13 percent

Not sure: 26 percent

Slightly disagree: 19 percent

Disagree: 31 percent

Illegal immigration is a moral issue, not a political or economic one.

Agree: 8 percent

Silghtly agree: 9 percent

Not sure: 12 percent

Slightly disagree: 20 percent

Disagree: 52 percent

July 13, 2006

2006 National Survey of Latinos

The Immigration Debate

by Roberto Suro and Gabriel Escobar, Pew Hispanic Center

Latinos are feeling more discriminated against, politically energized and unified following the immigration policy debate and the pro-immigration marches this spring, according to the 2006 National Survey of Latinos conducted by the Pew Hispanic Center.

More than half (54%) of Latinos surveyed say they see an increase in discrimination as a result of the policy debate, and three-quarters (75%) say the debate will prompt many more Latinos to vote in November. Almost two-thirds (63%) think the pro-immigrant marches this year signal the beginning of a new and lasting social movement. And a majority (58%) now believes Hispanics are working together to achieve common goals — a marked increase from 2002, when 43% expressed confidence in Latino unity.

The 2006 National Survey of Latinos was conducted by

telephone among a nationally representative sample of 2,000 Hispanic adults from June 5 to July 3, 2006. The survey has a margin of error of 3.8% for the full sample.

The survey shows that Latinos to some extent are holding the Republican Party responsible for what they perceive to be the negative consequences of the immigration debate, but the political impact of that perception is uncertain. Party affiliation among Latino registered voters has not changed significantly since the spring of 2004. However, the share of Latinos who believe the Republican Party has the best position on immigration has dropped from 25% to 16% in that time, with virtually the entire loss coming among foreign-born Hispanics (28% vs. 12%), who potentially represent an important and growing pool of future voters.

At the same time, the survey provides little solace for the Democratic Party, which showed no significant gains among Hispanic registered voters and which by some measures has lost some support. If anything, the survey shows that a growing number of Latinos are dissatisfied with both of the major parties.

Essay on Notes

Introduction

The announcement of the Census report in 2004 that Latinos are now the top minority in America only confirmed what many social demographers had already guessed. That unchecked illegal immigration and the higher birth rates for Latinos had drastically bumped up America's Latino population and that they had surpassed blacks in numbers. The Census report went beyond numbers, though, and talked about the profound social, economic and political changes the numbers meant for America from Jennifer Lopez becoming the nation's top earning entertainer to the surge in corporate ad dollars on Spanish language TV networks, "Hispanics Now Largest Minority," *CBS News,* January 21, 2003; "39 million make Hispanics largest U.S. minority," *USA Today,* June 19, 2003. Alphonso Pinckney in *The Myth of Black Progress* (New York: Cambridge University Press, 1984); William Julius Williams,

When Work Disappears: The World of the New Urban Poor (New York: Knopf, 1996); and Earl Ofari Hutchinson's, *The Crisis in Black and Black* (Los Angeles: Middle Passage Press, 1998) give an excellent analysis of the internal class divisions between the poor and the middle class within black America. For a general assessment of the social and political upheavals of the 1960s see Allen J. Matusow, *The Unraveling of America: A History of Liberalism in the 1960s* (New York: Perennial, 1985). Felix M. Padilla's *Latino Ethnic Consciousness: The Case of Mexican-Americas and Puerto Ricans in Chicago* (South Bend In.: University of Notre Dame Press, 1985) is a critical look at the history of relations between and identity conflicts among Mexican-Americans and Puerto Ricans in Chicago. Project 21 and the NAACP's wildly divergent positions on immigration are spelled out on their websites *NAACP.org* and *nationalcenter.og.*

There was a bit more to the story at Drew. The school was threatened with a massive federal fund cut-off, the loss of accreditation, and staff cuts. The outreach to Latinos was not an effort to appease federal funding agencies. However, the pressure from Washington was another spur that forced university administrators to recognize changes had to be made in the operations of the school, John L. Mitchell, "Drew University Reaches Out to Latinos," *LAT,* December 16, 2006.

Chapter 1

The surge in the Latino population and soaring num-

bers of illegal immigrants stirred a mix of fear and ambivalence among a wide segment of African-Americans. The
fear and ambivalence in turn sparked debate over what being number two among America's minorities meant for
blacks, Latinos and American society. New Orleans Mayor
Ray Nagin's quip about Mexicans and the Hispanic response
to it, "After Katrina: Continued Controversy," *en.wikipedia.
org/wiki/Ray Nagin* and "United States Hispanic Chamber of Commerce Deplores Remarks by New Orleans
Mayor Ray Nagin," *(HispanicPR Wire)* October 19, 2005.
The open letter penned in 2003 by Elizabeth Martinez sadly,
but not surprisingly, since it was not sensational news like
the headline "Latinos Now Number 1!" received almost
no media attention or commentary. Martinez, "Open Letter to African-Americans from Latinos," *Greater Diversity,
greaterdiversity.com/careerCR-2003/letter;*Rodriguez, "Black
and Tan Fantasy," May 30, 2001, *Salon, dir:salon.com/news/
feature;* "Hispanic Americans," *PBS, News Hour with Jim
Lehrer, March 16, 2001, puertorico-herald.org/issues/2001.*
The Selig Center for Economic Growth has closely tracked the
quantum leap in Hispanic wealth and consumer power since
the 1990s: "Hispanic buying power set to top all us minority
groups, report," on *nutraingredients-usa.com,* September 5,
2006. Anthony York details Bush's successful full-court press
to garner Latino support as Texas governor in the late 1990s
in "Bush's Latino Bid," *Salon.com/politics 2000/feature.* For

a recap of the 2004 presidential election results and Bush's Hispanic vote total, see "Bush 2004 Gains among Hispanics Strongest with Men," *National Annenberg Election Survey, Press Release*, December 21, 2004, *www.annebergpublicpolicycenter.org*, and for the affinity of Latino evangelicals for Bush and the GOP, see Jeff M. Sellers, "Hispanic Swing Vote Potentially Volatile," *Christianity Today*, February 10, 2003. The debate has raged among Latino writers and activists over who and what is a Hispanic or Latino, the divisions among the various Latino nationalities and the racial biases of the white-skinned Hispanics versus dark-skinned Hispanics: Marcelo M. Suarez-Orozco and Mariela M. Paez, "The Research Agenda" 1-37 in *Latinos: Remaking America* (Berkeley: University of California Press, 2002) and Jorge Ramos in *The Latino Wave* 96-103 (New York: Harper Collins, 2004), and Padilla in *Latino Ethnic Consciousness: The Case of Mexican-Americans and Puerto Ricans in Chicago* summarize the debate and its implications for race relations in America. Linda Chavez in *Out of the Barrio* (New York: Basic Books, 1991), 139-160 tells why she and others say Puerto Ricans are the exception to the immigrant making-it-in-America-rule. In Paulette Cooper's (ed.) *Growing Up Puerto Rican* (New York: Arbor House, 1972), a cross section of Puerto Rican-Americans give their personal narratives of life in America. They confirm and refute Chavez's contention that there's a "Puerto Rican Exception"; see also Nora Hamilton and Norma Stoltz (eds.), *Seeking Community in a Global City: Guatemalans and Salvadorans in Los Angeles* (Philadelphia: Temple University Press, 2001); Randy Ertll to Author, March 26, 2006. A worthwhile work on Dominican-Americans, the other South of the Border immigrant group often overlooked, but who have grown in numbers and have an impact on life in America's inner cities is R.R. Pesar's *A Visa for a Dream: Dominicans in the United States* (Boston: Allyn & Bacon, 1995). Houston Mayor Lee Brown's active courting of Hispanic voters in his mayoral run in 2001 paid off; see Salatheia Bryant, "Election 2001: Racial Pride to Play a Big Role in Runoff, *Houston Chronicle,* November 8, 2001. Paula D. McClain's survey of the negative attitudes of many Latino immigrants toward blacks in Durham opened up dialogue and debate about ethnic misconceptions many immigrants have of American blacks: "Scholars Ask Why Latinos View Blacks Poorly," *Diverse Online, divereeducation.com/artman,* July 12, 2006.

Chapter 2

Former Mexican President Vicente Fox never guessed that his remark about blacks and jobs would renew the colossal debate over race and racial stereotypes, but it did. See: Traci Carl, "Sharpton: Fox Must Apologize to Blacks," *AP,* May 21, 2005. The demand by the Congressional Hispanic Caucus, LULAC, MALDEF, and the National Council of La Raza that Fox apologize can be found in press releases on their respective websites: *Napolitano.house.gov/ chc/press releases; maldef.org, nclr.org, lulac.org/releases.* Fox, however, spoke for many Latinos who defended the president's remark: "Laurence Tiff and Lennox Samuels, "Fox remarks reflect Mexico's racial attitudes," *Dallas Morning News,* May 19, 2005; "Fox Apologizes for Comment That Mexicans in U.S. Do Work Blacks Won't," *freerepublic.com,* May 16. 2005. The Mexican stamp controversy came a month after the Fox flap, and that, along with the defense of the Memin Pinguin cartoon series by the Pinguin creator's daughter and other Mexicans, convinced more blacks that many Mexicans are racist: "Mexico Denies Stamps are Racist," *cbsnews.com,* June 30, 2005; Jan Tuckman explores caste and race divisions in Mexico in "Mexico's forgotten race steps into spotlight" in *The Guardian,* July 6, 2005, and so does Rachel Graves in "Forgotten Culture," *Houston Chronicle,* July 3, 2004. There are more details on race and caste in the country in "Afro-Mexican," *wikipedia.com.*

On the whiteness of foreign-born Hispanics, Tafoya reiterated a point that has been made time and again with every immigrant group that has come to America since the late 19th century. They have all rushed to identify as white men and women: "As an immigrant becomes more incorporated into the mainstream of U.S. society, they have a higher tendency to identify themselves as white. In some ways, it's intuitive." Not really: they understand that whites hold the wealth and power cards in America and that it's simply a pragmatic move for them to identify with those at the top, Genaro C. Armas, "Report says Hispanics personal racial ID goes beyond skin color in *Arizona Daily Star,* December 6, 2004. Michael Fletcher, "Latino Actors Cite Color Barrier in U.S.," *Boston Sunday Globe,* August, 2000; Henry Cisneros interview in Silvio Torres-Saillant, "Racial Diversity and Corporate Identity in the Latino Community" in *Latinos: Remaking America* 446; Marita Golden, *Don't Play in the Sun* (New York: Doubleday, 156-157). Gilberto Rincon and Bobby Vaughn are quoted in "Mexico's Fox Apologizes for Black Comment," *news.yahoo.com/s/mexico_fox_blacks,* May 16, 2005. The class and racial divisions are, as is well known, pernicious and long-standing in many Central and South American countries. The plight of blacks in many of these countries is dire. Ariel E. Dulitky makes a comprehensive study of their status in "A Region in Denial: Racial Discrimination and Racism in Latin America," *utexas. edu/law/academics/centers/human rights.*

Chapter 3

Time and again racial and ethnic stereotyping have resulted in disastrous public policy consequences, and that's no less true when it comes to Latinos and blacks. See Nicolas C. Vaca, *The Presumed Alliance* (New York: HarperCollins, 2004), 18. Vaca is not without his critics. Ed Morales brands

him and other Latino writers and activists who push a Latino first agenda as "Brownologists." Morales says that they
frown on coalition politics, and see black and brown relations as virtually permanently confrontational. This may be
unfair and overblown, but it's not an overstatement to say
that many Latinos are skeptical about the worth and prac-
ticality of forming alliances and coalitions with African-
Americans. They regard the differences between blacks and
browns as too great, and their interests too conflicting: Ed
Morales, "Brown Like Me?" in *The Nation,* March 8, 2004.
Chavez, *Out of the Barrio,* 188, and Patrick H. Mooney and
Theo J. Majka, *Farmers and Farm Workers Movements: Social Protest in American Agriculture* (New York: Twayne Publishers, 1995) detail the Bracero program and the Mexican
farmworkers' struggle against deportations. The Southern
Poverty Law Center, which tracks racial violence in the U.S.,
documents the attacks against immigrants in the U.S —from
harassment and threats to actual violence: *splcenter.org/intel/
intelreport/article,* Spring 2001.

CNN: "Minister Farrakhan Challenges Black Men," October 17, 1995, *cgi:cnn.com*; and Nelson Lim, "On the Back of
Blacks? Immigrants and the Fortunes of African-Americans,"
in Roger Waldinger (ed.), *Strangers at the Gates: New Immigrants in Urban America* (Berkeley: University of California
Press, 2001); Kwang Chung Kim (ed.), *Koreans in the Hood:
Conflict with African-Americans* (Baltimore: Johns Hopkins

University Press, 1999); Molly Hennessey-Fiske, "Immigrants who wire money get help from the Fed," *Los Angeles Times*, February 26, 2007; "Wells Fargo Considering Credit Cards for the Undocumented," *El Diario*, March 14, 2007. The Cuban economic and political miracle, and the Cuban refugees who sour relations with American blacks, is the subject of much analysis and ethnic agony: Alex Stepick and Carol Dutton Stepick, "Power and Identity: Miami Cubans" in Suarez-Orozco and Paez's *Latinos: Remaking America*, 75-92; Daryl Harris, "Generating Racial and Ethnic Conflict in Miami" in James Jennings (ed.), *Blacks, Latinos and Asians in Urban America* (Westport, Ct.: Praeger, 1994), and Vaca, *Presumed Alliance*, 108-126. Kwoh's quote was issued as a press statement condemning Kenneth Eng's hateful article, "Why I Hate Blacks," in *Asian Week*, February 23, 2007. Eric Harrison reports on the role of Latino cops in precipitating tensions with blacks in Miami: "Police, Cubans Blamed for Miami Riots," *LAT*, January 20, 1989. Ruiz and Valdes's saga told in the *New York Times* series, "How Race is Lived in America," "Best of Friends, Worlds Apart," *NYT*, June 5, 2000; Whitehead is quoted in Jennings, *Blacks, Latinos and Asians in Urban America*, 82. The account of the separate celebrations of white and black Cubans in Tampa is in *Latinos: Remaking America*, 436. Sam Dillon tells of the dismal economic conditions that force thousands of Mexicans to seek jobs and income in the

U.S. and its impact on Mexican society in "Smaller Families to Bring Big Change in Mexico," *NYT,* June 8, 1999. Mindiola Tatcho Jr., Yolanda Floes Niemann and Nestor Rodriguez (eds.) give a glimpse of the self-protective, circle the wagons clinging by many blacks to the legacy of the civil rights movement as their sole preserve in *Black-Brown Relations and Stereotypes* (Austin: University of Texas Press, 2003). Yet King, Abernathy, Coretta Scott King and Cesar Chavez were able to break through the narrowness of ethnic clinging and embrace each other in struggle: Chavez, "Lessons of Dr. Martin Luther King, Jr.," January 12, 1970; *Today in History,* August 22, 1970, *The American Library of Congress, American Memory Home Page.* Reggie White's outburst against Hispanics in "The Death of Reggie White: An Off the Field Obituary," *Public Affairs Magazine, politicalaffairs.net,* December 27-January, 2004; "Sharpton: Fox Must Apologize to Blacks," *AP,* May 21, 2005. The stereotypes of Latinos have been just as enduring and vicious as those of blacks: "Kingpin Reinforces Negative Stereotypes of Hispanics," *lulac.com*; Robert Klein, "Illegal Immigration and Black America," *San Francisco Chronicle,* May 26, 2004 (Tony Brown quote); "Stereotypes of Latinos," *wikipedia. org/wiki/stereotypes.* In a poll by the Public Policy Institute of California, nearly fifty percent of blacks said that immigrants (Latinos) were a burden on public services. Whites were evenly split on the issue: californiaprogressreport.com/2006/09/. Project 21 closely followed the conservative GOP script on immigration reform and lambasted illegal immigrants for allegedly creating a litany of social and economic ills: "African-American Group Assails Abuse of Entitlement Programs by Immigrants," *nationalcenter.org/press release*; Ak'Bar Shabazz, "Robbing Peter to Pay Pedro," *nationalcenter.org/shabazz immigration*. Immigrant rights groups point to countless reports such as Giovanni Peri's "How Immigrants Affect California Employment and Wages," California Counts, *Public Policy Institute of California*, February 2007 to rebut the accusations that immigrants are an economic drain on the economy and a burden to American taxpayers.

Chapter 4

When blacks and Latinos clashed at schools, and especially the jails in California, it sent out a frightening warning signal that violence, even racial hate violence, no longer is exclusively between whites and blacks. "Around the Nation: Hispanics and Blacks Clash in Florida Prison," *NYT*, January 11, 1982. It was the murderous brawls between Latinos and blacks in the Los Angeles County jails and California prisons that got the nation's attention: Megan Garvey and Richard Winton, "Critics of Jails Voice Alarm," *LAT*, February 14, 2006; Andrew Glazer, "Some gangs clash on race, not colors," *AP*, August 13, 2006; John Pomfret, "Jail Riots Illustrate Racial Divide in California," *Washington Post*, February 21, 2006.

The Latino and black gangs in New York City jails may not have been as sharply divided along ethnic lines as they are in California's jails, but there were violent encounters nonetheless: Frank Stroub and Paul E. O'Connell, "Why the Jails Didn't Explode," *City Journal,* Spring 1999. Tom Hayden in *Street Wars: Gangs and the Future of Violence* (New York: New Press, 2005) and James Diego Vigil in *Rainbow of Gangs: Street Culture in the Mega City* (Austin: University of Texas Press, 2002) give a solid history of and sound insights into Latino and black gang cultures in Los Angeles. The killing of Cheryl Green brought Los Angeles Mayor Antonio Villaraigosa, Los Angeles Police Department Chief William Bratton and a bevy of other city officials scurrying to the area, vowing to launch a gang crackdown: Sam Quinones, "How a Community Imploded," *LAT,* March 4, 2007. Many doubted that a crackdown on the violence in Harbor Gateway and in other parts of Los Angeles would be effective and saw the politicians' sudden involvement in the gang issue as simply photo-op pandering: Jeremiah Marquez, "A promised crackdown on gangs is met by skepticism," *Long Beach Press Telegram,* January 21, 2007. Annette Stark details the Highland Park killings and gang member convictions for them in "War of a Different Color," *City Beat,* March 8, 2007. Maria Louisa Tucker even suggested that the gang wars between blacks and Latinos were media contrived or at the very least blown out of proportion:

"The Myth of L.A.'s Race War," *Alternet*, February 24, 2006. The attacks on Latinos were assessed in Susy Buchanan, "The Rift: Evidence of a divide between blacks and Hispanics Mounting," *Intelligence Report*, Southern Poverty Law Center February 14, 2006, *splcenter.org*; *Hispanic Tips, hispanictips. com*, August 7, 2006. Los Angeles County hate crimes report: Susannah Rosenblatt, "Hate crimes up, study says," *LAT*, December 15, 2006. For the FBI's revealing investigation into the workings of the Mexican Mafia, see "Mexican Mafia," *foia/fbi.gov/foiaindex/mafia_mexican*; "Black-Hispanic Gang Rivalries Plague Los Angeles," *AP*, August 12, 2006. The university research study on stereotypes and ego reinforcement is in James Waller, *Face to Face: The Changing State of Racism Across America* (New York: Insight Press, 1998); Michael A. Fletcher, "Biggest Bigots: Often It's Minorities," *WP*, April 7, 1998; Randal C. Archibold, "Racial Hate Feeds a Gang War's Senseless Killing," *NYT*, January 17, 2007.

Chapter 5

Though the jail clashes in California were the biggest and the bloodiest, it wasn't the only place where Latinos and blacks occasionally clashed. The jockeying over what kind of education blacks and Latinos want for their children was also a crucial point of contention. See: Buchanan, "The Rift" on school clashes nationally, *Intelligence Report*, February 14, 2006, SPLC. Joel Rubin and Nicholas Shield report extensively on the Jefferson High School flap: "School Official to Step Down," *LAT,* June 1, 2005, and Peter Skerry details the Cooke School dispute over bilingual education: "The Black Alienation," *New Republic,* January 30, 1995. Cathleen Decker reports on the 'English only" and anti-bilingual education ballot success in California and black support of it: "Bilingual Education Ban Widely Supported," *LAT,* April 13, 1998; "What Works? Reviewing the Latest evidence on Bilingual Education" in *Language Learner,* November/December 2005. Semanticist and later U.S. senator S.I. Hayakawa, who founded the organization U.S. English in 1983, and Linda Chavez in *Out of The Barrio,* 9-38, are both from immigrant backgrounds, and were the earliest and best-known proponents of the "English only" movement. Surveys show the overwhelming majority of Latino parents see bilingual education as the path to English proficiency, "Five Immigration Myths Exploded", American Immigration Lawyers Association, *aila.org,* and "Results of a Nationwide Survey of Hispanics," *Catholic News Service,* May 6, 2005, *jknirp. com.* Gingrich also realized that his "ghetto" gaffe could also sink his long-shot rumored entrance into the 2008 presidential sweepstakes. That was even more reason that he scrambled fast to "clarify" his remark, "Gingrich clarifies bilingual 'ghetto' remark: " *USA Today,* April 5, 2007. For the differing views of some blacks and Latinos on the importance of desegregation, see Amy Stuart Wells, "Hispanic Education in America: Separate and Unequal," *ERIC Digest* No. 59, 1989. The companion civil rights and school desegregation fights that Mexican-Americans waged before and during the 1960s are detailed in Vaca, *Presumed Alliance*, 62-84, and Ruben Donato, *The Other Struggle for Equality: Mexican-Americans during the Civil Rights Era* (Albany: SUNY Press, 1997). The Civil Rights Project at Harvard University (now at UCLA) has been relentless in documenting the re-segregation of America's big city schools: "A Multiracial Society with Segregated Schools—-Are We Losing the Dream?" January 16, 2002, *civil rightsproject.Harvard.edu*. The school funding gap between rich and poor school districts continues to widen every year, and the federal government hasn't helped matters: Amit R. Paley, "Program Widens School Funding Gap, Report Says," *WP*, December 21, 2006. A blowback from under resourced poor urban schools is the chronically high dropout rate of blacks and Latinos: Duke Helfand, "Nearly Half of Blacks, Latinos Drop Out, School Study Shows," *LAT*, March 25, 2005; Courtney Cavaliere, "Black caucus opposes education reform bill," *The Daily Texan*, March 9, 2005, *dailytexanonline.com*.

Chapter 6

The political battlefield at times also proved to be a fertile field for both conflict and cooperation between blacks and Latinos. But while many Latinos anticipated big gains politically, some blacks viewed those gains with apprehension. They feared that they'd come at their expense and they would diminish their relatively new-found political clout. Bush and the GOP's and the Democrat's massive courting of the Latino vote didn't ease their fears, Kelly Wallace: "Bush, Democrats court Hispanics with bilingual radio ads," May 5, 2001, *cnn.com/2001*. The Democrats and Bush certainly turned on the campaign money spigot: Marisa Trevino, "For Latino voters, best years ahead," November 10, 2006, *usatoday.com/oped*; Adam Segal, "Record $9 Million Spent on Spanish-language TV Campaign Ads," October 29, 2002, *hispanicbusiness.com/news*, and Viveca Novak, "Translating Faith into Spanish," October 25, 2004, *time.com*. "The Latino Vote in the 2004 Election" gives a complete analysis of the impact of the vote at, *Political Science online, apsanet.org*; also see Michael Barone, "Latino Voters and American Politics," *U.S. News & World Report*, October 10, 2002, *usnews.com/usnews/opinion/baroneweb*; and Frank Morris and James G. Gimpel, "Immigration, Intergroup Conflict, and the Erosion of African-American Political Power in the 21st Century," 7, February 2007, *cis.org/articles*. And for the impact of the swelling immigration population on big cities, see "Census: Immigrants stabilize big-city populations," *cnn.com/2007/us/04/05.metro.population.ap*.

Latino political groups increasingly are making proactive use of the 1965 Voting Rights Act and have taken the lead in the fight to enforce its provision on bilingual ballots: Melanie Eversley, "For a Mississippi town, Voting Rights Act made a change," *USA Today,* August 5, 2005. The spectacular leap in the number of Latino elected officials and Latino voters was the talk of the nation in the presidential elections of 2004 and raised the eyebrows of top Democrats and Republicans even higher: see Daniel B. Wood, "Latino politicians gain clout in U.S.," *Christian Science Monitor,* May 19, 2006; Arian Campo-Flores and Howard Fineman, "A Latin Power Surge," May 30, 2005, *msnbc.com*; Thomas B. Edsall and Zachary A. Goldfarb, "Bush is Losing Hispanics' Support," *WP,* May 21, 2006; Janet Hook, "A Hard Line Could Erode Latino Vote," *LAT,* March 28, 2006; Carolyn Lochhead, "Demographics Fuel GOP's Immigration Dilemma," *San Francisco Chronicle,* April 4, 2006; Genaro C. Armas, "Report says Hispanics personal racial ID goes beyond skin color," in *Arizona Daily Star,* December 6, 2004.

The loss of Latino support would be a disaster for the GOP, especially with the growing national influence of Latino elected officials: "LULAC Hails Record Latino Voter Turnout," November 4, 2004, *lulac.org/advocacy/press2004*; The 2004 National Survey of Latinos: Politics and Civic Participation, July 2004, Pew Hispanic Center, *pewhispanic.org*. California Governor Arnold Schwarzenegger pulled out all stops to seduce Latino voters in the 2003 recall and 2006 elections: "Schwarzenegger Attempting to Woo Latino Voters Through Hispanic Media," *La Opinion*, July 27, 2006. The modest slack-off in the number of black elected officials was an issue of concern to the Joint Center: "Number of Black Male Elected Officials Declining," December 3, 2003, *Joint Center for Political and Economic Studies, jointcenter.org/ pressroom*. Bush tried to take full advantage of black's disaffection with the Democrats in 2004: "Bush tries to sow doubts about Democrats in Urban League Address," *Detroit News*, July 26, 2004. Black voters, though, had more doubts about him than the Democrats. See "Fact Sheet, The Hispanic Electorate in 2004," *Pew Hispanic Center, pewhispanic.org/files*. While Hispanic Republican elected officials were a rare breed, they still posed a countervailing force to the Hispanic Democrats and gave Republicans a political wedge with a substantial number of Latino voters. That was enough to keep Republicans on their toes when it came to addressing the needs of Latino voters: "The Congressional Hispanic Conference," *hace-usa.org*; Ramos, *The Latino Wave*, 161 (Bonilla quote).

Despite the GOP election debacle in the 2006 midterm elections, Bush's political guru Karl Rove still had a core of Latino political operatives such as Texas ad executive Lionel Sosa and the new chair of the Republican National Committee, Mel Martinez, to push the GOP's pro-family values, pro-religion, anti-abortion, anti-gay marriage and pro-business agenda, and these issues still resonated with many Latinos: Roberto Novato, "The Ascent of the

New Latino Right," spring 2007, Vol.21 No.2, *publiceye.org.*
The Dellums-Fuente Oakland mayoral bout was a relatively
civil, even gentile affair. It showed that two veteran politicians could compete without resorting to ethnic nastiness in
a city lightly divided on ethnic lines, Christopher Heredia,
"Ethnic support won't be enough in Oakland race," *San Francisco Chronicle*, June 4, 2006; "Coronado Project Selects Plus
Threes," May 31, 2005 *Hispanic PR Wire;* Teresa Watanabe
and Nicole Gaouette, "Next: Converting the Energy of Protest to Political Clout," *LAT,* May 2, 2006.

Chapter 7

Can viable black and Latino political coalitions be built,
and more importantly, sustained? Los Angeles Mayor Antonio Villaraigosa appeared to show that it could be done in Los
Angeles, a city that's been intensely balkanized by race. But
did he really? Or was it, as one Latino political observer called
it, a "romantic image?"; Betty Pleasant, "Blacks in a Quandry
Over L.A. Mayor's Race," August 6, 2004, *Wave Newspapers.*
Frank Morris and James G. Gimpel give a decidedly negative
view of ethnic coalitions, and contend that such coalitions don't
work and harm blacks: "Immigration, Intergroup Conflict and
the Erosion of African American Political Power in the 21st
Century," February 2007, *Center for Immigration Studies, cis.
org/articles*. But the authors have a political ax to grind. They
are unabashed immigration reform foes and CIS operatives.

The Villaraigosa loss in 2001 and subsequent win in 2005 was a textbook example of how a Latino politician bent over backward to overcome black fears of Latino political domination at city hall: Vaca, *Presumed Alliance*, 85-107; Erin Texeira, "Generation Gap Seen in Black Support for Hahn," *LAT*, May 27, 2001; and George Skelton, "Affection for Hahn a Hurdle Villaraigosa Couldn't Vault," *LAT*, June 7, 2001; "A Latino Power Surge," May 30, 2005, *msnbc. Com*; Morris, et.al., "Immigration, Intergroup Conflict...." is on firmer ground in his concise and detailed assessment of the demographic changes in south Los Angeles and what that means for the future of black elected officials locally and in Congress from that area (Dymally quote), 21. John Mitchell, "Black Politicians See New Landscape in L.A. Politics," *LAT*, August 4, 2006. Ellis Cose, "Black Versus Brown," *Newsweek*, July 3-10, 2006. Vaca discusses the Ferrer and Green contest and Ferrer's failure to get key black political endorsements: *Presumed Alliance*, 183; also see "New York Mayoral Election," *turnstile.cssny. org/turnstile/mayoralelection* (nd); "U.S. Rep Luis Gutierrez joins Daley bandwagon," February 13, 2007 *hispanictips.com*. Though there were few public displays of unity such as joint press conferences, press statements or public meetings by and between the two legislative groups, the CHC and the CBC appeared to march in lockstep on the crucial public policy issues. For a sampling of the vital issues that concerned both groups, see their press releases: *napolitano.house.gov/*

chc/news, and *cbcfinc.org* ; "Baca Receives an 'A' Grade from NAACP on Voting Record," *house.gov/apps/list/press*. The complete NAACP legislative report card on the 109th Congress is in *The Crisis*, March/April 2007, 45-48.

Chapter 8

The saying is that there's nothing new under the sun. That's certainly the case with the immigration debate. The debate raged among blacks for more than a century and a half before Congress made immigration reform an issue in 2006. Towering black historical figures, from Frederick Douglass to Marcus Garvey in the 19th and early 20th Centuries, weighed in on it. In almost every instance the leaders were harsh in their views of immigrants and their affect on blacks; the concern was always jobs. The quotes on immigration from the black historical figures and the black press are found in "Robert Malloy, "Cast Down Your Bucket Where You Are: Black Americans on Immigration," *Center for Immigration Studies Paper #10*, June 1996. Phillip S. Foner provides the most complete history and assessment of the conflicts between black workers, white unions and immigrants in the U.S. in *History of the Labor Movement in the United States* (New York: New World Paperbacks, 1972) and *Organized Labor and the Black Workers, 1619-1973* (New York: Praeger Publishers, 1974). Jennings, *Blacks, Latinos, and....*" 151, 152 (Ringer and Leiberson quotes). For a summary of the 1924 Immigration Act and its racist intent see, Immigration Act of 1924, *answers.com/ topic/immigration-act-of-1924*; Madison Grant, *The Passing of the Great Race, or the Racial Bias of European History* 1916 (New York: Ayer Co., reprint 1970). The subtitle tells a reader all they need to know about the prevalent view of much of the American public that Europeans, i.e. Germans, Scandinavians and the English were the master race and all others including Italians, Greeks, Spaniards and Portuguese were inferiors and thus posed a threat to American racial purity. They had to be barred from America.

Chapter 9

No issue has inflamed black opinion on immigration more than the issue of jobs. Namely, do illegal immigrants take jobs from blacks? The pros and cons of this have been fiercely fought over before, during and after the great immigration battle in Congress in 2006. Blacks, of course, have been the centerpiece of that fight and have been agonizingly split on it, Carroll Doherty: "Attitudes Toward Immigration: in Black and White," April 26, 2006, *Pew Research Center, pewresearch.org*. Leslie Fulbright, "Polls, Leaders say many blacks support illegal immigrants," *SF Chronicle*, April 13, 2006. Jackson has spoken frequently on the issue of immigration and jobs: Rachell L. Swarms, "Growing Unease for Some Blacks on Immigration," *NYT*, May 4, 2006. Dan Stein of the

Federation for American Immigration Reform immediately disputed the National Academy of Sciences Report on Immigration, *NYT*, May 18, 1997 in a letter to the *NYT*, May 25, 2007, "Report Oversells Immigration's Meager Benefits." The Center for Immigration Studies has churned out volumes that purport to show the dire harm of immigration to the American economy and life. They're all on their website, *cis.org*; Stephen Ohlemacher, "Study: Up to 12 million illegal immigrants in US; efforts to stem flow have not slowed pace," *AP*, March 8, 2006. Borjas and his study was a hot-ticket item in the press during the immigration debate in 2006: George Borjas, "Increasing the Supply of Labor Through immigration," May 2004, *immigrationonline.org/research*; Darryl Fears, "Blacks conflicted about immigration debate," *WP*, April 8, 2006; Nell Henderson, "Effect of Immigration on Jobs, Wages is Difficult for Economists to Nail Down," *WP*, April 15, 2006; Carolyn Zaayer, "Economists Disagree on Immigrant Employment Puzzle," *Fox News*, December 13, 2005, *foxnews.com*. Many blacks still do work in lower-end jobs: M.L. Ingram, "Are Illegal Immigrants Taking Jobs from Blacks?," *Philadelphia Tribune*, April 10, 2006. The debate over immigration and jobs spilled over into demands by Latinos to get a bigger share of public sector jobs. The debate was sharpest in L.A. County. The GAO Study and Tirso's complaint about the under-representation of Latinos in the post office are cited in Skerry, "The Black Alienation,"

New Republic, July 1995. For an assessment of the vitriol between black and Latino employee groups in L.A. County over
who gets the jobs, and the equally long and fierce fight by
blacks to get jobs and promotions in municipal agencies, see
Jerry Yaffe, "Discrimination Against Hispanics in the Public Sector Work Force," *Journal of Intergroup Relations 20,
no.1, 1993,* 39-50; Phillip I. Moss, "Employment gains by minorities, women in large city government, 1976-83," *Bureau
of Labor Statistics,* November, 1988, *bls.gov/opub/mlr/1988.*
The National Urban League has documented in its annual reports the still gaping lag in everything from income to health care between blacks and whites: Erin Texeira, "Study: Blacks Still lag Whites," *AP,* March 29, 2006;
Alec Klein, "A Tenuous Hold on the Middle Class," *WP,*
December 18, 2004 (Spriggs quote); Daniel B. Wood, "Rising black-Latino clash on jobs," *CSM,* May 25, 2006 (Ertll
quote) and Texeira, "Blacks concerned legalizing undocumented immigrants hurts workers," *AP,* April 6, 2006.
For a full account of the lawsuits by blacks alleging discrimination against them in favor of Latinos, see Miriam Jordan,
"More blacks claim they are passed over for Latinos in hiring,"
Wall Street Journal, January 24, 2006; Anderson's statements
on his view of the affect of illegal immigration on blacks are
on the Harvest Institute website, "Immigration Harms Black
America," *harvestinstitute.org/immigration_pr_2006pdf.*
Former NAACP President Bruce Gordon walked the tight-

rope on the immigration and jobs controversy in an interview with Black America Web: Michael H. Cottman, "NAACP, Barack Obama Call for Earned Citizenship for Illegal Immigrants," April 3, 2006, *blackamericaweb.com.*

Chapter 10

The immigration-versus-black-jobs-loss conflict can be fine-tuned even more to examine the impact of illegal immigration on industries where poor, unskilled young blacks work. In some of these industries blacks have lost ground to illegal immigrants. But is that due to porous immigration policies and enforcement, or discrimination? This opens up a fresh area of controversy. Sheila Jackson-Lee conveyed some ambivalence on this question in an interview with Black America Web: Michael H. Cottman, "The State of Black America, Part 2, "The Nation's Debate Over Illegal Immigration and How it Impacts Us," January 17, 2007, *blackamericaweb.com*; Teresa Watanabe, "Blacks, Latinos Seek Common Ground on Divisive Issues," *LAT,* May 5, 2006. The Sentencing Project has done a thorough job of annually documenting the astronomically high incarceration rate of young black males and its cost to society: *sentencingproject. org*; "The Crisis of Black Male Joblessness," March, 2007; *Fact Sheet, Senate Joint Economic Committee,* Dirksen Senate Office Building, Washington, DC 20510; "May Jobless Rate for African-Americans a Dismal 10.1 Percent," Congressional

Black Caucus, June 3, 2005, *congressionalblackcaucus.net*. The criminalization of wide segments of young black males and its troubling consequences continues to be well documented by researchers, Devah Pager: "The Mark of a Criminal Record," *AJS Journal*, Volume 108, Number 5, March 2003, 937-75; "Many New York employers discriminate against minorities, ex-offenders," *News Release*, April 1, 2005, *Princeton. edu/main/news/archives*; Alan B. Krueger, "Employers discriminate against blacks," *NYT*, December 12, 2002; Joleen Kirschenman and Kathryn M. Neckerman, "We'd Love to Hire Them But….": The Meaning of Race for Employers" in Christopher Jencks and Paul Peterson (eds.), *The Urban Underclass* (Washington, D.C.: Brookings Institution Press, 1991); Renee D. Turner, "Black jobs recovery on life support," April 29, 2004, *bet.com*; Jerry Seper, "Arrival of aliens ousts U.S. workers at Katrina Coast," *Washington Times*, April 10, 2006. In the fight over clean-up jobs in New Orleans and the Gulf Coast, black immigration opponents pointed to the ill treatment of Mexican workers by contractors to make their point another way that if the jobs had gone to blacks, the abuses wouldn't have happened. This is a dubious point: "One Year Later: Many Gulf Coast Residents Victimized by Companies Hiring Illegal Immigrants," August 25, 2006, *chooseblackamerica.com/ press*; "Lawsuits Filed by Post-Katrina Construction Workers," July 17, 2006, *npr.org*; the BLS survey is cited by the Center for Immigration Studies, September 2006, *cis.org/articles*.

The joint organizing effort by the SEIU is detailed in Stephen Lerner, "Black-Brown Unity," *Urban Habitat,* spring 2007, on *urbanhabitat.org*; Hazel Trice Edney, "Immigration Could Unite or Divide Blacks, Hispanics," *Sacramento Observer,* March 2, 2004.

Chapter 11

In what has to be one of the strangest alliances in living memory, at the height of the battle over immigration a core of black activists linked up with conservatives, some with checkered ties to avowed racist groups. The issue, of course, was stopping illegal immigration at the border and in Congress. The author was among those invited to participate in the FAIR-backed press conference by anti-immigration blacks in D.C. The invitation was extended, based on a series of articles that I wrote on the immigration fight and blacks. Many of the participants I knew personally, and in a few cases had worked with on justice and racial discrimination issues. I respected their work in these areas, but parted company with them in their one-dimensional view of the immigration contest. I felt there was much danger that they could be used to further pit blacks against Latinos. Keyonna Summers, "Black leaders oppose alien amnesty plan," *Washington Times,* May 24, 2006; "Choose Black America," SourceWatch, (undated) *sourcewatch.org*. For Choose Black America's hard line attacks on immigration reform see their press statements at *chooseblackamerica.com/press*; see FAIR's website, *fairus.org*. The alliance with the handful of blacks who sported Minuteman Project tee shorts and boasted of their membership in the group seemed even odder, but they were there. The website of Stormfront contains the blatant race-baiting rants of fringe white supremacist groups on immigration, *stormfront.org*; Anti-Defamation League Report, "Ku Klux Klan Rebounds with New Focus on Immigration," February 6, 2007, *adl.org/prerelease/extremism*. For a hyper-critical interpretation of the black-Minuteman connection, see Brentin Mock, "Smokescreen," *Intelligence Report*, Fall 2006, Southern Poverty Law Center, *splcenter.org/intel*, and for a benign interpretation of the connection see the Minuteman Project website, *minutemanproject.com* and "Black Activists Join to March with Minutemen," April 23, 2006, *CBS News, cbs2.com*; Diversity Inc. staff, "Why Some Blacks Reject the Immigration Movement," May 4, 2006, *diversityinc.com*. Blacks again apparently gave majority support to Arizona's anti-immigration proposition 200: News Max staff, "Blacks, Hispanics, Poor Favor Immigration Crackdown," April 1, 2006, *newsmax.com*. Project 21 quickly jumped back into the immigration fray, and this time loudly declared that immigration reform was not a civil rights issue: "Black Activists say Immigration Shortcuts are a not a Civil Rights Issue," May 1, 2006, *nationalcenter.org*. Immigration rights activists were greatly amused by the flap between Stewart and Gil-

christ, but Stewart's ascension to the top spot in the organization was one more sign that some blacks could be as rabid
against immigration reform as conservative whites, maybe
even more so: "Black Minuteman Assaulted by Columbia
University Mob," October 13, 2006, *minutemanproject.com*;
Gillian Flaccus, "Minuteman Project embroiled in leadership
dispute," *AP*, February 27, 2007.

Chapter 12

Next to the inflaming issue of jobs, the other issue that
punched the hot button of many blacks was the comparison
of the immigrant rights movement to the 1960s black-led
civil rights movement. Mainstream civil rights organizations
were guardedly supportive of the comparison, black conservatives and a wide segment of the black public vehemently
disagreed. This opened up another fresh area of debate, not
only on immigrant rights as a legitimate civil rights struggle, but underneath, the tensions between blacks and Latinos over whether they were and are true allies in the civil
rights struggle: Contreras's quote in Swarms, "Growing Unease for Some Blacks on Immigration," *NYT*, May 4, 2006.
See Ronald Reagan's statement on signing the Immigration Reform and Control Act of 1986. *reagan.utexas.edu/
archives/speeches/1986*; The parameters of the Congressional
immigration reform bill and the deep soul search it sparked
in the GOP twenty years after Reagan signed the 1986 bill

are in Gail Russell Chaddock's "A GOP faceoff over illegal immigration," *CSM*, March 29, 2006. Drake Bennett points up the divisions that the immigration battle stirred in the NAACP in "Fence Sitters," *Boston Globe*, April 9, 2006. The Immigration reform bill of 1986; Clarence Page, "For black workers, history is repeating itself," *Newsday*, May 27, 2005. The impressive, even spectacular organizing efforts of the immigration marches were driven in great part by Spanish language radio station DJs: "Spanish-Language Media Organized Protests," *AP*, March 28, 2006; Eduardo Stanley, "a las calles," To the Streets!, *National Catholic Reporter*, April 7, 2006. The National Council of La Raza was stung by the charge that it had been less than vigorous in the overall civil rights battles; it answered critics in a detailed fact sheet on its civil rights activities in "The Truth About NCLR: NCLR Answers"; see the websites of MALDEF and LULAC for press statements on their respective efforts on non-immigration related civil rights issues, *maldef.org/fair/index and lulac.org/advocacy*. See also *NAACP Mission Statement, naacp.org/about* and *mapa.org/aboutus;* For Dymally's views on immigration reform and his mild irritation at taking a back seat role on the immigration rights battle, see his website *democrats.assembly.ca.gov/members/a52/newsroom.*

Taylor Branch gives a full-bodied analysis of the personalities, politics and history of the March on Washington in *Parting the Waters: America in the King*

Years, 1954-63 (New York: Simon & Schuster, 1988). Deneen Moore echoed Project 21's official anti-immigration reform and civil rights stance, May 1, 2006, *nationalcenter. org/P21PRImmigrationAmnesty.* The NAACP laid out a pro-active, supportive stance on immigration reform in March 2006: Michael H. Cottman, "NAACP, Barack Obama Call for Earned Citizenship for Illegal Immigrants," *Black America Web*, April 3, 2006, *blackamericaweb.com.*

Chapter 13

The instant American troops set foot into Iraq in March 2003, a majority of African-Americans said that they opposed the war. In part they opposed it because it was Bush's war, and anything that was associated with the Bush administration was anathema to most blacks. They also opposed it because there was the overwhelming sense that it was a no-win war and that more blacks would die in the war than whites. The same polls, though, showed that a majority of whites initially backed the war. The surprise to some was that a majority of Latinos backed it too: Justin Berton, "Latinos enlisting in record numbers," *SF Chronicle*, May 15, 2006. The soaring enlistment numbers was helped along by gargantuan spending by the U.S. Army on paid advertisements on Univision and other Spanish language TV stations, imploring Latinos to join up and be all that you can be in the military: *bloomberg.com/apps/news.* The war divide was now a divide in black and white, and black and Latino, too. This was yet another new development in ethnic relations, Terry M. Neal: "Bush, Blacks and Iraq," *WP*, May 20, 2004. Robert B. Edgerton presents a concise history of blacks in America's Wars in *Hidden Heroism: Black Soldiers in America's Wars* (Boulder: Westview Press, 2001). Wallace Terry wrote the classic soldier's story book on the suffering and disillusionment of black troops in Vietnam: *Bloods: An Oral History of the Vietnam War* (New York: Presidio Press, 1985). The Pew Hispanic Center tracked Latino attitudes toward the war from initial enthusiasm to opposition, "Fact Sheet: Latinos and the War in Iraq," January 4, 2007, *pewhispanic.org*. John P. Schmal gives a good survey of the ignored and minimized Latino contribution to America's wars: "Hispanic Contributions to America's Defense," November 11, 1999, *houstonculture.org/Hispanic/memorial*. Controversy over Hispanic battlefield sacrifices and historians' continued blind-spot to it raged when Hispanic groups protested that filmmaker Ken Burns made no mention of the half-million U.S. and foreign-born Latinos who had fought in World War II and the eleven Mexican-American and two Puerto Rican Medal of Honor winners in his seven part PBS documentary, on World War II, "The War" Dick Kreck, "Latinos left out of 'The War'," *Denver Post,* March 4, 2007. Michael H. Cottman, "The War at Home—What the Invasion of Iraq is Costing us Stateside," State of Black America, Part 3, January 1, 2007, *blackamericaweb.com.* By late 2004,

Latinos overwhelmingly had begun to voice discontent about the war, yet still retained their unwavering loyalty to the military: Richard Morin and Dan Balz, "Most Latinos Say Iraq War was Wrong," *WP*, October 28, 2004; Raul Reyes, "Latinos know up close the cost of Iraq war," *USA Today*, January 19, 2007; Cottman, "The War at Home...." (Cheeks-Kilpatrick quote).

Conclusion

Dr. King's vision was that the Poor People's March in 1968 would be a mighty effort to unite the poor of all colors and ethnic groups in a titanic battle against poverty. From the start there was discord. That stemmed not just from the disorganization, lack of funds, or poorly defined means to attain the objective by March organizers. There was also infighting and jealousy over who should lead the March. Some in King's inner circle were adamant that blacks should lead it and that all others should take a back seat in the March: all others included Latinos. That threatened to if not derail the March, certainly taint it: Robert T. Chase, "Class Resurrection: The Poor People's Campaign of 1968 and Resurrection City," *Essays in History, University of Virginia, Volume Forty, 1998*. The effort by MALDEF and Jackson to effect a coalition on justice and civil rights issues is spelled out in MALDEF issued press releases, May 18-19, 2005, *maldef.org/news/press*.

The effort, sadly, seemed to die a quiet death. Conference organizers in Los Angeles, for at least one day, seemed to fare better. They were able to pull off a conference. That held the promise of a future for those determined to make black and Latino unity more than a politically correct cliché: Teresa Watanabe, "Blacks, Latinos Seek Common Ground on Divisive Issues" (Durazo and Chavez Quotes), *LAT*, May 5, 2006.

Bibliography

Andrews, George Reid. *Afro-Latin America, 1800-2000* (New York: Oxford University Press, 2004)

Aptheker, Herbert. *A Documentary History of the Negro people in the United States: From the Reconstruction Years to the Founding of the NAACP in 1910* (New York: The Citadel Press, 1968)

Billington, Ray A. *The Protestant Crusade: 1800-1860: A Study of the Origins of American Nativism* (Gloucester, Mass.: Peter Smith, 1963)

Borjas, George J. "Do Blacks Gain or Lose from Immigration?" in Daniel S. Hamermesh and Frank D. Bean. (eds.) *Help or Hindrance the Economic Implications of Immigration for African-Americans* (New York: Russell Sage Foundation, 1998)

Borjas, George J. *Heaven's Door: Immigration Policy and the American Economy* (Princeton, N.J.: Princeton University Press, 2001)

Chavez, Linda. *Out of the Barrio* (New York: HarperCollins, 1991)

Chinchilla, Norma and Hamilton, Nora. *Seeking Community in a Global City: Guatemalans and Salvadorans in Los Angeles* (Philadelphia: Temple University Press, 2001)

Cooper, Paulette (ed.) *Growing Up Puerto Rican* (New York: Arbor House, 1972)

Conrad, Cecilia A and Whitehead, John, et.al (eds) *African Americans in the U.S. Economy* (New York Rowman & Littlefield Publishers, 2005)

DeGevova, Nicholas. *Working the Boundaries: Race, Space, and Illegality in Mexican Chicago* (Durham, NC: Duke University Press, 2005)

De Genova, Nicholas. *Latino Crossings: Mexicans, Puerto*

Ricans and the Politics of Race and Citizenship (New York: Routledge, 2003)

Dzidienyo, Anani and Oboler, Suzanne. *Neither Enemies nor Friends: Latinos, Blacks, and Afro-Latinos* (New York: Palgrave Macmillan, 2005)

Erie, Steven. "Rainbow's End: From the Old to the New Ubran Ethnic Politics" in Lionel Maldonado and Joan Moore (eds) *Urban Ethnicity in the United States: New Immigrants and Old Minorities* (Beverly Hills, Ca.: Sage Publications, 1985)

Feagin, Joe R. and Melvin P. Sikes. *Living With Racism: The Black Middle-Class Experience* (Boston: Beacon Press, 1994)

Foner, Phillip S. *Organized Labor and the Black Workers, 1619-1973* (New York: Praeger Publishers, 1974)

Franklin, John Hope. *From Slavery to Freedom* (New York: Random House, 1967)

Frederickson, George M. *The Black Image in the White Mind: The Debate on Afro-American Character and Destiny, 1817-1914* (New York: Harper & Row, 1971)

Gomes, Ralph C. and Williams, Linda Faye (eds) *From Ex-*

clusion to Inclusion: The Long Struggle for African American Political Power (Westport, Ct.: Greenwood, 1992)

Gutierrez, David G. *The Columbia History of Latinos in the United States Since 1960* (New York: Columbia University Press, 2004)

Guttman, Herbert. *The Black Family in Slavery and Freedom, 1750-1925* (New York: Vintage Books, 1976)

Hall, Gwendolyn Midlo. *Slavery and African Ethnicities in the Americas* (Chapel Hill, NC: University of North Carolina Press, 2006)

Harris, Abram L. and Spero, Sterling D. *The Black Worker* (New York: Columbia University Press, 1959 (reprint 1931)
Hayden, Tom. *Street Wars: Gangs and the Future of Violence* (New York: New Press, 2004)

Higham, John. *Send These to Me: Jews and Other Immigrants in Urban America* (New York: Atheneum Press, 1975)

Holzer, Harry J. *What Employers Want: Job Prospects for Less-Educated Workers* (New York: Russell Sage Foundation, 1996)

Jennings, James (ed). *Blacks, Latinos, and Asians in Urban America* (Westport, Ct.: Praeger, 1994)

Jennings, James (ed). *The Politics of Black Empowerment* (Detroit: Wayne State University, 1992)

Mann, Robert. *The Walls of Jericho: Lyndon Johnson, Hubert Humphrey, Richard Russell, and the Struggle for Civil Rights* (New York: Harcourt, Brace & Company, 1996)

Meier, August. *Negro Thought in America, 1880-1915* (Ann Arbor, Mi.: University of Michigan Press, 1968)

Mendez, Rodenas Adriana and Mendez, Adriana. *Cubans in America* (Minneapolis, Mn.: Lerner Publishing, 1994)

Mindiola, Tatcho Jr. *Black-Brown Relations and Stereotypes* (Austin, Tx.: University of Texas Press, 2003)

Nelson, William E. and Perez-Monforti, Jessica (eds). *Black and Latina/o Politics: Issues in Political Development in the United States* (Miami: Barnhardt and Ashe Publishing, Inc., 2006)

Padilla, Felix. *Latino Ethnic Consciousness: The Case of Puer-*

to Ricans and Mexicans in Chicago (Indianapolis: University of Notre Dame Press, 1985)

Paez, Mariela M., Suarez-Orozco, Marcelo M. *Latinos: Remaking America* (Berkeley, Ca. University of California Press, 2002)

Ramos, Jorge. *The Latino Wave* (New York: HarperCollins, 2004)

Reed, Ishmael (ed) *MultiAmerica* (New York: Viking Press, 1997)

Robinson, Randall. *The Debt: What America Owes Blacks* (New York: Dutton, 2000)

Sansone, Livio. *Blackness Without Ethnicity: Constructing Race in Brazil* (New York: Palgrave Macmillan, 2003)

Sawyer, Mark Q. *Racial Politics in Post-Revolutionary Cuba* (New York: Cambridge University Press, 2005)

Suro, Roberto and Singer, Audrey. Latino Growth in Metropolitan America: Changing Patters, New Locations Center on Urban and Metropolitan Policy and the Pew Hispanic

Center, July 2002 (Washington D.C.: The Brookings Institution Survey Series, Census 2000)

Torres-Saillant, Silvio. "Visions of Dominicanness in the United States," in Frank Bonilla (ed.) *Borderless Borders: U.S. Latinos. Latin America and the Paradox of Interdependence* (Philadelphia: Temple University Press, 1998)

Vaca, Nicolas C. *The Presumed Alliance: The Unspoken Conflict between Latinos and Blacks and what it means for America* (New York: HarperCollins, 2004)

Velez-Ibanez, Carlos G. *Border Visions: Mexican Cultures of the Southwestern United States* (Tucson: University of Arizona Press, 1996)

Wade, Peter. *Race and Ethnicity in Latin America* (New York: Pluto Press, 1997)

Waldinger, Roger (ed.). *Strangers at the Gates: New Immigrants in Urban America* (Berkeley, Ca.: University of California Press, 2001)

Waller, James. *Face to Face: The Changing State of Racism Across America* (New York: Insight Books, 1998)

Whalen, Carmen Teresa and Vazquez-Hernandez, Victor. *The Puerto Rican Disapora: Historical Perspectives* (Philadelphia: Temple University Press, 2005)

Wilson, William Julius. *When Work Disappears: the World of the New Urban Poor* (New York: Knopf, 1996)

Yun, Grace. *Intergroup Cooperation in Cities: African, Asian and Hispanic American Communities* (New York: Asian-American Federation of New York, 1993)

Index